Inflation Targeting

Inflation Targeting

Why the value of money matters to you

JOHN BAIDEN, B.Sc., MBA, M.Sc.
(distinction), JD, LL.M (distinction)
Central University College, Ghana

To order additional copies of this book, contact:
Xlibris Corporation
1-888-795-4274
www.Xlibris.com
Orders@Xlibris.com
108745

CONTENTS

EXECUTIVE SUMMARY

This book happens to be the author's treatise on inflation and his thesis on Inflation Targeting. The book discusses the remedies for inflation in general and 'inflation targeting' in particular.

The book is divided into four chapters. Chapter one covers what is inflation, causes of inflation and how inflation is measured. Inflation is an increase in the average level for all goods and services, usually measured by changes in the consumer price index and the GDP deflator. There are different economic schools of thought as to the causes of inflation. The two most prevalent theories are neo-classical (Monetarist View), which postulates that inflation is caused by increases in money supply, often used to finance government spending and Neo-Keynesian view which posits that inflation is the result of diminishing returns of productivity.

Chapter Two discusses why inflation matters. Inflation matters because it is 'bad news'. It not only distorts prices but erodes savings, discourages investment, stimulates capital flight (into foreign assets, precious metals or unproductive real estate), inhibits growth, makes economic planning uncertain, and in its extreme form, brings about social and political unrest therefore various governments find ways and means of containing it by adopting conservative and sustainable fiscal and monetary policies. In the past, Central banks attempted to wrestle inflation by targeting monetary aggregates or exchange rates. With time, these intermediate targets were thought of as ineffective. Now, the new approach to the age-old problem of controlling inflation is known as Inflation Targeting. It was first practiced in New Zealand in 1990. Currently there are 22 countries practicing inflation targeting, otherwise called "Inflation Targeting Regimes".

Chapter three delves into what inflation targeting is, other techniques of controlling inflation, models of inflation targeting and advantages cum disadvantages of inflation targeting. Inflation targeting is a monetary policy in which a Central Bank estimates and makes public, a projected or 'target' inflation rate and then attempts to steer actual inflation towards the target through the use of interest rate changes and other monetary tools that can be used to affect money supply. It is 'Responsible Central Banking'. In its best practice, it gives a central Bank independence from political interference while making the central bank responsible for effectively containing inflation. Inflation targeting framework provides a clearly defined nominal target, a coherent approach to decision making, the flexibility to respond to unanticipated shocks, and a strategy for communicating with the public and financial markets. Inflation targeting track record is rather short. There is no concrete record to situations where adhering to an inflation target will be detrimental to economic performance. Case studies done on industrialized inflation targeting regimes reveal reductions in both inflation and its expectations thereof. These countries have also experienced both an increase in output growth and a reduction in output volatility relative to the experience of non-inflation targeting countries.

Chapter Four ends the research with my analysis and conclusion of theoretical and empirical findings of Inflation and Inflation Targeting. I was persuaded by three major case studies done mostly by eminent economists of the U.S. Federal Reserve System, including the current chairman Ben Bernanke, rendering inflation targeting as a very successful approach to Monetary Policy. Combining the overwhelming successes of inflation targeting framework by the countries within the case study with Keynesian Macro-economic theory of Consumption and Investment Function, which posits more consumption and investment spending in low inflation economies, I take the position that "Inflation targeting not only enhances the effectiveness of Monetary Policy but also stabilizes rate of inflation, economic growth, and employment".

CHAPTER ONE

INFLATION

Inflation is an economic condition characterized by a rise in the level of prices for all goods and services and declining purchasing power as measured against some baseline of Purchasing Power. (Case, Fair 2004)

A careful distinction should however be made between what "inflation" is from a rise in price or price increase for specific good. Inflation is an increase in the average level of prices, not a change in any specific price, but an average change in price level for all goods and services, usually measured by changes in the Consumer Price Index (CP) and the GDP deflator.

Inflation for workers is a sustained increase in the general level of prices when workers salaries or remuneration are not rising by the same rate. The effect of this is diminished purchasing power.

Inflation has been among the more serious economic problems of the world during the past half century, with many nations experiencing far higher annual rates of inflation than those currently prevailing in the United States. (Rose, Marquis. 2006). In year 2000, the inflation rate in the Democratic Republic of Congo for example was 554%, Angola 32% and Japan -0.6% (www.imf.org).

The effect of high inflation is diminished purchasing power, relative high cost of living, low savings and investments, which can lead to unemployment, low standard of living and social unrest. These adverse consequences of inflation have made inflation fighting a predominant focus for most governments and central banks. According to Fredric S. Mishkin (a former Governor of the Federal Reserve Bank), Price Stability is the Macroeconomic mission of the Federal Reserve Board (Mishkin, 2007).

In New Zealand, the Governor of the Reserve Bank of New Zealand must sign a Policy Target Agreement with the Minister of Finance agreeing not to get inflation over 3% in the medium term. The governor has inflation target range of 1-3% annually. The governor could be technically prosecuted or removed from office if the inflation target is not achieved. (www.rbnz.govt.nz)

CAUSES OF INFLATION

There are different economic schools of thought as to the causes of inflation. The two most prevalent theories are the neo-classical theory (Monetarist View), which postulates that inflation is caused by increases in money supply, often used to finance government spending and the Neo-Keynesian view which posits that inflation is the result of diminishing returns of Productivity.

THE MONETARIST VIEW

The monetarist view rests on the quantity theory of money. They assert that empirical study of monetary history shows that "inflation is always and everywhere a monetary phenomenon".

The Quantity Theory of Money, simply stated, is that the total amount of spending in an economy is primarily determined by the total amount of money in existence. From this theory the following formula is created:

$$P = Do/So$$

Where P is the general price level of consumers' goods. Do is the aggregate demand for consumers' goods and So is the aggregate supply of consumers' goods. The idea behind this formula is that the general price level of consumers' goods will rise only if the aggregate supply of consumers' goods goes down relative to the aggregate demand for consumers' goods, or if the aggregate demand increases relative to the aggregate supply of consumers' goods. Based on the idea that total spending is based primarily on the total amount of money in existence. Economists calculate aggregate demand for consumers' goods based on the total quantity of money. Therefore, they posit that as the quantity of money increases, total spending increases and the aggregate demand for consumers' goods increases as well. For this reason the economists who believe in the Quantity Theory of Money also believe that the only cause for rising prices in a growing economy (this means aggregate supply of consumers' goods is increasing), is an increase of the total quantity of money in existence, which is caused by central bank monetary policies, often not pegged to any commodity that will constrain their printing and creation of money.

NEO—KEYNSAIN THEORY

The Neo-Keynesian economic theory presents three types of inflation, as part of what Robert J. Gordon calls the "triangle model" (faculty-web.at.nwu.edu/economics/Gordon/indexlayers.html).

- ❖ **DEMAND PULL INFLATION**—inflation due to high demand for goods /services and low unemployment, also known as Phillips Curve inflation.
- ❖ **COST-PUSH INFLATION**—Currently termed "supply shock inflation", due to an event such as a sudden increase in the price of oil from global market

forces. Producers for whom oil is part of their cost are very likely to increase the prices of their Outputs. Cost-push can also come for labor demand for increased wages and salaries.

❖ **BUILT-IN INFLATION**—This is induced by adaptive expectations. Often linked to the "price/wage spiral" because it involves workers trying to keep their wages up with prices and then employers passing higher costs on to consumers as higher prices as part of a "vicious circle". Built-in inflation reflects events in the past, and so might be seen as hangover inflation. It is also known as "inertial" inflation, "inflationary momentum", and "structural inflation" .

These three types of inflation can be added up at any time to get an explanation of the current inflation rate. However, over time, the first two (and the actual inflation rate) affect the amount of built-in inflation: persistently high (or low) actual inflation leads to higher (lower) built-in inflation.

The neo-classical use the Phillips curve to explain the relationship between inflation and employment. This means some amount of inflation is needed to increase employment or reduce unemployment.

The Philips Curve is said to have described the U.S experience well in the 1960's but failed to describe the combination of rising inflation and economic stagnation (stagflation) experienced in the 1970's. As a result, the Phillips curve has been deemed to represent only the demand pull component of the triangle model. Increases in aggregate demand drives price upwards and this motivates suppliers to produce more, thereby utilizing more labor.

Keynesians by contrast to the monetarists, emphasize the role of **aggregate demand** in the economy rather than

money supply in determining inflation. Aggregate demand for the Keynesian, is a function of so many variables **of which money supply is only one** of the variables. These variables are interplay of internal market forces such as population growth (demographics), innovation, money supply, spending patterns, external shocks such as wars, weather, and trade disruptions, and policy levers such as tax, budget and regulatory decision.

Another Keynesian concept is the potential output (sometimes called the "natural gross domestic products"), a level of GDP where the economy is at its optimal level of production, given institutional and natural constraints. This level of output corresponds to the NAIRU or the "natural" rate of unemployment or the full-employment unemployment rate. In this framework, the built-in inflation rate is determined endogenously (by the normal workings of the economy). If GDP exceeds its potential (and unemployment is below the NAIRU), the theory says that, all else equal, inflation will accelerate as suppliers increase their prices and built-in inflation worsens. This causes the Phillips curve to shift in the stagflation direction, toward greater inflation and greater unemployment. This kind of "inflationary acceleration" may have been seen in the late 1960s in the U.S, when Vietnam War spending (counteracted only by small tax hikes) kept unemployment below 4% for several years.

If GDP falls below its potential level and unemployment is above the NAIRU, all else equal inflation will decelerate as suppliers attempt to fill excess capacity, cutting prices and undermining built-in inflation: there is disinflation. This causes the Phillips curve to shift in the desired direction, towards less inflation or less unemployment. This disinflation may have been seen in the early 1980s, when Fed chief Paul Volker's anti-inflation campaign kept unemployment high for several years and at almost 10% for two years. If GDP is equal to potential (and the unemployment rate equals the NAIRU), the inflation rate will not change, as long as there are no supply shocks. In the "long run", most neo-Keynesians see the Phillips Curve as vertical. That is the unemployment is given and equal to the NAIRU, while there are a large number of possible inflation rates that can prevail at that unemployment rate. However, one problem with this theory for policy-making purposes is that the exact level of potential output (and of the NAIRU) is generally unknown and tends to change over time. Inflation also seems to work in an asymmetric way, rising more quickly than it falls.

Most non-Keynesian theories of inflation can be understood within the neo-Keynesian perspective as assuming that the NAIRU and potential output are both unique and are attained relatively quickly. With the "supply side" at a fixed level, the amount of inflation is determined by aggregate demand. The fixed supply side also implies that government and private-sector spending are always in conflict, so that government deficit spending leads to crowding out of the private sector and has no effect on the level of employment. Thus, it is only money supply and monetary policy that determine the inflation rate, as a result of **aggregate demand exceeding aggregate supply, therefore inflation**.

For these reasons neo-Keynesian theory focuses on productivity, because it is falling productivity, which signals diminishing returns of production, and therefore inflationary pressures from overheating and output above 'potential'. From the neo-Keynesian perspective budget balancing and restraints on spending do not control inflation, and persistent budget deficits do not control inflation. What causes inflation is an increase in velocity of money, and the reduction in efficiency caused by excessive present consumption versus investment.

That is savings rate that is too low to fund the improvements in production required to keep pace with increases in aggregate demand. Consequently neo-Keynesians such as Franco Modigliani warned that it is an insufficient savings rate which is the better predictor of future inflation.(Case, Fair 2004).

RATIONAL EXPECTATIONS

The Rational Expectation School (Rashex) posits that economic actors look into the future and try and maximize their general sense of future state of well-being and do not simply respond to the immediate opportunity cost and pressures of the present. In this view, while, generally grounded in monetarism, future expectations and strategies are important for inflation as well.

One fundamental assertion of Rashex is that actors will seek to "head off" central bank decisions, by preemptively engaging in inflationary behavior. This means that central banks must establish their credibility in fighting inflation, or have economic actors make bets that the economy will expand, believing that the central banks will expand the money supply rather than allow a recession which would be very damaging to the economy, and possibly require government bailouts. In this view central banks might be at an advantage renouncing some flexibility of monetary policy, in order to persuade economic actors that the central bank will not allow inflation.

THE AUSTRIAN SCHOOL

The Austrian School's view on Inflation is based on the writings of Ludwig Von Misses, Fredrich von Hayek and Murray Rothbard. They advocated that money must be denominated in a stable unit of account, against which other prices are measured. This, in other words is the support for a gold standard of a very strict variety when all notes are convertible on demand to gold.

In the Austrian view, inflation is equivalent to an increase in the money supply. In this view price changes only represent inflation if they are driven by monetary effects, whereas price changes, whether up or down, that do not correlate to monetary effects are merely the workings of the market mechanism. Inflation only becomes harmful in the Austrian view if changes in the money supply are spurred by central banking authorities and not necessarily by the actions of miners under a commodity standard.

In this framework, there is a real rate of inflation, which is based on the money supply and the real rate of interest. Price fluctuations are measured against this real rate of inflation, to determine whether the money supply is being expanded above real potential output. In the Austrian view both the 1920s and the 1990s saw "inflation" because of increases in the money supply, even though price levels were relatively stable. This means inflation of the money supply does not necessarily manifest itself in an **increase in the general price** level but can instead manifest itself in an **increase in the prices of specific goods** or assets due to an increased demand for these goods caused by the creation of new money. The price of these specific goods going up or down depends on how the **new money** enters the economy and the **preference of the actors**. In essence their emphasis is that inflation manifest itself in the changes of specific prices that producers and consumers who have received the inflated money first purchase. Therefore changes in general price levels are not necessary to witness true inflation.

The Austrian school also views deflation as positive, because it shows that the same level of real production can be accomplished at a lower expenditure of scare resources. Falling prices because of lower costs of production is seen as improving standards of living, rather than a threat to real output. They refer to this as "growth deflation."

The Austrians don't believe in the Phillips Curve. They think inflation and unemployment are not mutually exclusive. Thus inflation can still ensue and there may not be a change in unemployment or a reduction in unemployment.

THE MARXIST VIEW

In the Marxist view, value is based on the labor required to extract a given commodity versus the demand for that commodity by those with money. Marxist view is related to other "classical" economic theories that argue that monetary inflation is caused solely by printing notes in excess of the basic quantity of gold. However, Marx argues that the real kind of inflation is in the cost of production measured in labor. Because of the classical labor theory of value, the only factor that is important is whether more or less labor is required to produce a given commodity at the rate it is demanded.

SUPPLY-SIDE SCHOOL

The supply-siders assert that inflation is always caused by either an increase in the supply of money or a decrease in the demand for money. The value of money is seen as being purely subject to these two factors.

Thus the inflation experienced during the Black Plague in medieval Europe is seen as being caused by a decrease in the demand for money (the money stock used was gold coin and it was relatively fixed), whilst the inflation of the 1970s is regarded as initially caused by an increased supply of money that occurred following the US exit from the Bretton Woods gold standard. Supply-side economics asserts that the money supply can grow without causing inflation as long as the demand for money also grows.

INFLATION MEASUREMENTS

Regardless of the probable cause(s) of inflation, inflation is agreed by most economists as either continuous price increases or continuous falling value of money, which can be measured.

Various indexes have been devised to measure different aspects of inflation. The CPI measures inflation as experienced by consumers in their day-to-day living expenses; the Producer Price Index (PPI) measures inflation at earlier stages of the production and marketing process; the Employment Cost Index (ECI) measures it in the labor market; the BLS International Price Program measures it for imports and exports; and the Gross Domestic Product Deflator (GDP Deflator) measures combine the experience with inflation of governments (Federal, State and Local), businesses, and consumers. Finally, there are specialized measures, such as measures of interest rates and measures of consumers' and business executives' expectations of inflation.

The "best" measure of inflation for a given application depends on the intended use of the data. The CPI is generally the best measure for adjusting payments to consumers when the intent is to allow consumers to purchase at today's prices, . basket of goods and services equivalent to one that they could purchase in an earlier period. The CPI also is the best measure to use to translate retail sales and hourly or weekly earnings into inflation-free dollars. (stats.bls.gov/cpifeg.htm).

CONSUMER PRICE INDEX (CPI)

The Consumer Price Index (CPI) is a measure of the average change over time in the prices paid by urban consumers for a market basket of consumer goods and services.

The CPI affects nearly all Americans because of the many ways it is used. Following are major uses:

As an economic indicator.
As a deflator of other economic series
As a means of adjusting dollar values.

The CPI reflects spending patterns for each of two population groups: all urban consumers and urban wage earners and clerical workers. The all-urban consumers group represents about 87 percent of the total U.S population. It is based on the expenditures of almost all residents of urban or metropolitan areas, including professionals, the self-employed, the poor, the unemployed and retired persons as well as urban wage earners and clerical workers. Not included in the CPI are the spending patterns of persons living in rural non-metropolitan areas, farm families, persons in the Armed Forces, and those in institutions, such as prisons and mental hospitals. The price change experience of the all urban consumer group is measured by two indexes, namely the traditional Consumer Price Index for All Urban Consumers (CPI-U) and the newer Chained Consumer Price Index for All Urban Consumers (C-CPI-U).

The CPI-W is based on the expenditures of households included in the CPI-U definition that also meet two requirements: More than one-half of the household's income must come from clerical or wage occupations and at least one of the household's earners must have been employed for at least 37 weeks during the previous 12 months. The CPI-W's population represents about 32 percent of the total U.S population and is a subset, or part, of the CPI-U's populations.

The CPI frequently is called a cost-of-living index, but it differs in important ways from a complete cost-of-living measure. BLS has for some time used a cost-of-living framework in making practical decisions about questions that arise in constructing the CPI. A cost-of-living index is a conceptual measurement goal, however, not a straightforward alternative to the CPI. A cost-of-living index would measure changes over time in the amount that consumers need to spend to reach a certain utility level or standard of living. Both the CPI and a cost-of-living index would reflect changes in the prices of goods and services, such as food and clothing that are directly purchased in the marketplace; but a complete cost-of-living index would go beyond this to also take into account changes in other governmental or environmental factors that affect consumers' well-being. It is very difficult to determine the proper treatment of public goods, such as safety and education, and other broad concerns, such as health, water quality, and crime that would constitute a complete cost-of-living framework.

It is important to understand that BLS bases the market baskets and pricing procedures for the U and W populations on the experience of the relevant average household, not on any specific family or individual. It is unlikely that one's experience will correspond precisely with either the national indexes or the indexes for specific cities or regions. A national average reflects all the ups and down of millions of individual price experiences. It seldom mirrors a particular consumer's experience.

The CPI market basket is developed from detailed expenditure information provided by families and individuals actually bought. For the current CPI, this information was collected from the Consumer Expenditure Survey over the two years 2001 and 2002. In each of those years, about 10,000 families from around the country provided information on their spending habits in a series of quarterly interviews. To collect information on frequently purchased items such as food and personal care products, another 7,500 families in each of the 2 years kept diaries listing everything they bought during a 2-week period.

Altogether, more than 30,000 individuals and families provide expenditure information for use in determining the importance, or weight, of the more than 200 categories in the CPI index structure.

The CPI represents all goods and services purchased for consumption by the reference population (U or W) BLS has classified all expenditure items into more than 200 categories, arranged into eight major groups. Major groups and examples of categories in each are as follows:

FOOD AND BEVERAGES (breakfast cereal, milk coffee, chicken, wine, service meals and snacks)

HOUSING (rent of primary residences, owners' equivalent rent, fuel oil, bedroom furniture)

APPAREL (men's shirts and sweaters, women's dresses, jewelry)

TRANSPORTATION (new vehicles, airline fares, gasoline, motor vehicle insurances)

MEDIAL CARE (prescription drugs and medical supplies, physicians' services, eyeglasses and eye care, hospital services)

RECREATION (televisions, pets and pet products, sports equipment, admissions);

EDUCATION AND COMMUNICATION (college tuition, postage, telephone services, computer software and accessories);

OTHER GOODS AND SERVICES (tobacco and smoking products, haircuts and other personal services, funeral expenses).

Also included within these major groups are various governments—charged user fees, such as water and sewerage charges, auto registration fees, and vehicle tolls. In addition, the CPI includes taxes (such as sales and excise taxes) that are directly associated with the prices of specific goods and services. However, the CPI excludes taxes (such as income and Social Security taxes) not directly associated with the purchase of consumer goods and services.

The CPI does not include investments items, such as stocks, bonds real estate, and life insurance. (These items relate to savings and not to day-to-day consumption expenses)

For each of the more than 200 item categories, using scientific statistical procedures, the Bureau has chosen samples of several hundred specific items within selected business establishments frequented by consumers to represent the thousands of varieties available in the marketplace. For example, in a given supermarket, the Bureau may choose a plastic bag of golden delicious apples, U.S extra fancy grade, weighing 4.4 pounds to represent the Apples category.

Each month, BLS data collectors called economic assistants visits or call thousands of retail stores, service establishments, rental units, and doctors' offices, all over the United States to obtain information on the prices of the thousands of items used to track and measures price changes in the CPI. These economic assistants record the prices of about 80,000 items each month representing a scientifically selected sample of the prices paid by consumers for the goods and services purchased.

During each call or visit, the economic assistant collects price data on a specific good or service that was precisely defined during an earlier visit. If the selected item is available, the economic assistant records its price. If the selected item is no longer available, or if there have been changes in the quality or quantity (for example, eggs sold in packages of 8 when they previously had been sold by the dozen) of the good or service since the last time prices had been colleted, the economic assistant selects a new item or records the quality change in the current item.

The recorded information is sent to the national office of BLS where commodity specialists who have detailed knowledge about the particular goods or services priced review the data. These specialists check the data for accuracy and consistency and make any necessary correction or adjustments which can range from an adjustment for a change in the size or quantity of a packaged item to more complex adjustments based upon statistical analysis of the value of an item's features or quality. Thus, the commodity specialists strive to prevent changes in the quality of items from affecting the CPI's measurement of price change. (stats.bls.gov/cpi)

HOW IS THE CPI CALCULATED?

The CPI is a product of series of interrelated samples. First, using data from the 1990 Census of Population, BLS selected the urban areas from which data on prices were collected and chose the housing units within each area that were eligible for use in the shelter component of the CPI. The Census of Population also provided data on the number of consumers represented by each area selected as a CPI price collection area. Next, another sample (of about 16,800 families each year) served as the basis for a Point of-Purchase Survey that identified the places where households purchase various types of goods and service.

Data from the Consumer Expenditure Survey conducted in 2001 and 2002, involving a national sample of more than 30,000 information families, provided detailed information on respondents' spending habits. This enabled BLS to construct the CPI market basket of goods and services and to assign each item in the market basket a weight, or importance, based on total family expenditures. The final stage in the sampling process is the selection of the specific detailed item to be priced in each outlet. This is done in the field, using a method called disaggregation. For example, BLS economic assistants may be directed to price "fresh whole milk." Through the disaggregation process, the economic assistant selects the specific kind of fresh whole milk that will be priced in the outlet over time. By this process, each kind of whole milk is assigned a probability of selection, or weight, based on the amount the store sells. If for example, vitamin D, homogenized milk in half-gallon containers makes up 70 percent of the sales in whole milk and the same milk in quart containers accounts for 10 percent of all milk sales, then the half-gallon container will be seven items as likely to be chosen as the quart container. After probabilities are assigned, one type, brand, and size container of milk is chosen by an objective selection process based on the theory of random sampling. The particular kind of milk that is selected by disaggregation will continue to be priced each month in the same outlet.

In sum, the price movement measurement is weighted by the importance of the item in the spending patterns of the appropriate population group. The combination of all these factors gives a weighted measurement of price change for all items in all outlets, in all areas priced for the CPI.

Certain taxes are included in the CPI, namely, taxes that are directly associated with the purchase of specific goods and services (such as sales and excise taxes). Government user fees are also included in the CPI. For example, toll charges and parking fees are included in the transportation category and an entry fee to a national park would be included as part of the admissions index. In addition, property taxes should be reflected indirectly in the BLS method of measuring the cost of the flow of services provided by housing shelter, which we called owner's equivalent rent, to the extent that these taxes influence rental values. Taxes not directly associated with specific purchases, such as Income and Social Security taxes, are excluded, as are the government services paid for through those taxes.

For certain purposes, one might want to define price indexes to include, rather than exclude, income taxes. Such indexes would provide an answer to a question different from the one to which the present CPI is relevant, and would be appropriate for different uses.

HOW INDEX IS INTERPRETED

An index is a tool that simplifies the measurement of movements in numerical series. Most of the specific CPI indexes have a 1982-84-reference base. That is, BLS sets the average index level (representing the average price level) for the 36-month period covering the years 1982, 1983 and 1984 equal to 100. BLS then measures changes in relation to that figure. An index of 110, for example, means there has been a 10-percent increase in price since the reference period; similarly an index of 90 means a 10 percent decrease. Movements of the index from one date to another can be expressed as changes in index points (simply, the difference between index levels), but it is more useful to express the movements as percent changes. This is because the level of the index in relation to its base period affects index points, while percent changes are not.

In the table that follows, item A increase by half as many index points as item B between Year I and Year II, yet because of the different starting figures, both had the same percent change; that is, price advanced at the same rate. By contrast, items B and C show the same change in index points, but the percent change is greater for item C because of its lower starting value.

	Item A	Item B	Item C
Year I	112.5	225.0	110.0
Year II	121.5	243.0	128.0
Change in index points	9.0	18.0	18.0

Percent change 9.0/112.5 x 100 = *8.0* *18.0/225.0 x 100 =* **8.0**
18.0/110.0 x100 = **16.4**

Historically, BLS has updated its reference periods every 10 years or so.

The foregoing can be represented using the following relationship:

$$\Delta P = \frac{(P1t-P1t-1)}{Pt1-1} \times 100$$

Where ΔP is the percentage in prices or in the price index between two time periods (t and t-1), P1t is the price or price index in period t, and P1t-1 is the price index in the previous time period (t-1).

With the above example using the just stated formula, Item A will be:

$$\frac{(121.5-112.5)}{112.5} \times 100 = 8\%$$

To determine what has happened to Purchasing Power, the relationship is the ff:

Purchasing Power of the U.S dollar = $\frac{1}{\text{CPI for P1t}} \times 100$

So for Item A, it will be:

$$\frac{1}{121.5} \times 100 = .82$$

This means one dollar of the base period (P1t-1) is eighty two cents current period (P1t).

LIMITATIONS OF THE CPI

The CPI is subject to limitations in application and limitation in measurement.

LIMITATIONS IN APPLICATION.

The CPI may not be applicable to all population groups. For example, the CPI-U is designed to measure the experience with price change of the U.S urban population and thus may not accurately reflect the experience of people living in rural areas. Also, the CPI does not produce official estimates for the rate of inflation experienced by subgroups of the population, such as the elderly or the poor. (BLS does produce and release an experimental index for the elderly populations; because of the significant limitations of this experimental Index, it should be interpreted with caution.)

The CPI cannot be used measure difference in the levels or living cost between one place and another; it measures only time-to-time changes in each place. A higher index for one area does not necessarily mean that prices are higher there than in another area with a lower index. It merely means that prices have risen faster since the two areas common reference period.

The CPI cannot be used as a measure of total change in living costs because changes in these costs are affected by (such as social and environmental changes and changes in income taxes) that are beyond the definitional scope of the index and so are excluded.

LIMITATIONS IN MEASUREMENT

Limitations in measurement can be grouped into two basic types, sampling errors and non-sampling errors.

SAMPLING ERRORS: Because the CPI measures price change based on a sample of items, the published indexes differ somewhat from what the results would be if actual records of all retail purchases by everyone in the index population could be used to compile the index. These estimating or sampling errors are limitations on the precise accuracy of the index, not mistakes in calculating the index. The CPI program has developed measurements of sampling error, which are updated and published annually in the CPI Detailed Report. An increased sample size would be expected to increase accuracy, but it would also increase CPI production costs. The CPI sample design allocates the sample in a way that maximizes the accuracy of the index, given the funds available.

NON-SAMPLING ERRORS: These errors occur from a variety of sources. Unlike sampling errors, they can cause persistent bias in the measurement of the index. Non-sampling errors are caused by problems of price data collection, logistical lags in conducting surveys, and difficulties in defining basic concepts and their operational implementation, and difficulties in handling the problems of quality change. Non-sampling errors can be far more hazardous to the accuracy of a price index than sampling errors. BLS expends much effort to minimize these errors. Highly trained personnel ensure the comparability of quality of items from period to period; collection procedures are extensively documented. The CPI program has an ongoing research and evaluation program, to identify and implement improvement in the index.

PRODUCER PRICE INDEXES

In addition to the familiar Consumer Price Index, there are three Produce Price Indexes (PPIs). The PPIs keep track of average prices received by producers. One index includes crude materials, another covers intermediate goods, and the last covers finished goods. The three PPIs don't include all producer prices but primarily those in mining, manufacturing, and agriculture. Like the CPI, changes in the PPIs are identified in monthly surveys.

Over long periods of time, the PPIs and the CPI generally reflect the same rate of inflation. In the short run, however, the PPIs usually increase before the CPI, because it takes time for producers' price increases to be reflected in the prices that consumers pay. For this reason, the PPIs are watched closely as a clue to potential changes in consumer prices.

THE GDP DEFLATOR

The broadest price index is the GDP deflator. The GDP deflator covers all output, including consumer goods, investment goods, and government services. Unlike the CPI and PPIs, the GDP deflator isn't based on a fixed "basket" of goods or services. Rather, it allows the contents of the basket to change with people's consumption and investment patterns. The GDP deflator therefore isn't a pure measure of price change. Its value reflects both price changes and market responses to those price changes, as reflected in new expenditure patterns. Hence, the GDP deflator typically registers a lower inflation rate than the CPI.

The deflator is derived by dividing the current period (P1t) CPI by the base Index, typically 100.

A deflator is used to derive Real GDP. It is in essence the percentage to reduce current prices to get the equivalent price in a previous period.

Real vs. Nominal GDP- The GDP deflator is used to adjust nominal output values for changing price levels. Nominal GDP refers to the current-dollar value of output, whereas real GDP denotes the inflation-adjusted value of output. These two measures of output are connected by the GDP deflator.

For example if the nominal values of GDP were $10 trillion in 2000 and $5.7 trillion in 1990. However, the price level rose by 24 percent between those years. Hence, real GDP in 2000 in the base-period prices of 1990 was

$$\text{2000 real GDP (in 1990 prices)} = \frac{\text{nominal GDP}}{\text{price deflator}} = \frac{\$10 \text{ trillion}}{\frac{124}{100}} = \frac{\$10 \text{ trillion}}{1.24}$$

$$= \$8.06 \text{ trillion}$$

Changes in real GDP are a good measure of how output and living standards are changing. Nominal GDP statistics, by contrast, mix up output and price changes.

CORE INFLATION

Core inflation is measure of inflation that excludes certain items that face volatile price movements.

The preferred measure by the Federal Reserve of core inflation in the United States is the core Personal consumption expenditures price index. This is based on chained dollars.

Since February 2000, the Federal Reserve Board's semiannual monetary policy reports to congress have described the Board's outlook for inflation in terms of the PCE. Prior to that, the inflation outlook was presented in terms of the CPI. In explaining its preference for the PCE, the Board stated: The chain-type price index for PCE draws extensively on data from the consumer price index but, while not entirely free of measurement problems, has several advantages relative to the CPI. The PCE chain-type index is constructed from a formula that reflects the changing composition of spending and thereby avoids some of the upward bias associated with the fixed-weight nature of the CPI. In addition, the weights are based on a more comprehensive measure of expenditures. Finally, historical data used in the PCE price index can be revised to account for newly available information and for improvements in measurements techniques, including those that affect source data from the CPI; the result is a more consistent series over time.

The core PCE price index measure also has proved to be more accurate and consistent in measuring and predicting inflation over the Consumer Price Index. It makes room for hedonic adjustments and deliberately excludes volatile goods.

The older preferred measure of inflation in the United States was the Consumer Price Index. This is still used as the indicator for most other countries, and is presented monthly in the US by the Bureau of Labor Statistics. This index tends to change more on a month-to-month basis than does "core inflation." This is because core inflation eliminates products that can have temporary price shocks (i.e. energy, food products). Core inflation is thus intended to be indicator and predictor of underlying long term inflation.

Robert J. Gordon introduced the concept of core inflation as aggregate price growth excluding food and energy in a 1975 paper. This is the definition of "core inflation" most used for political purposes.

CHAPTER TWO

WHY INFLATION MATTERS

Inflation makes a society determine who is hurt and who is helped. Although inflation makes some people worse off, it makes other people better off. This constitutes redistribution of income and wealth. Consistent high inflation therefore has a profound influence on a society's economic welfare and social cohesion.

By altering relative prices, incomes, and the real value of wealth, inflation turns out to be a mechanism for redistributing incomes and wealth. The redistributive mechanics of inflation include

- **Price effects.** People who prefer goods and services that are increasing in price least quickly end up with a larger share of real income. (Schiller, Bradley R., 2003)
- **Income effects.** People whose nominal incomes rise faster than the rate of inflation end up with a larger share of total income.
- **Wealth effects.** People who own assets that are increasing in real value end up better off than others.

On the other hand people whose nominal incomes don't keep peace with inflation end up with smaller shares of total output. The same thing is true of those who enjoy goods that are rising fastest in price or who hold assets that are declining in real value. In this sense, inflation acts just like a tax, taking income or wealth from one group and giving it to another. But we have no assurance that this particular tax will behave like Robin Hood, taking from the rich and giving to the poor. In reality, inflation often redistributes income in the opposite direction. When the Mexican government ended it long standing subsidy of tortillas on Jan 1, 1999, Mexico witnessed a major political backlash (demonstration and civil disobedience) particularly among impoverished Mexican who rely on the soft, chewy disks for half of their daily diet (Anderson, 1999).

According to Arthur Okun, an economist credited with Okun's Law" a significant real cost of inflation is what it does to morale, to social coherence, and to people's attitude towards each other. He adds that this society is built on implicit and explicit contracts that are linked to the idea that the dollar means, something. If you cannot depend on the value of the dollar, this system is undermined. People will constantly feel they've been fooled and cheated (Okun, 1978)

Psychotherapists report that **"inflation stress"** leads to more frequent marital spats, pessimism, diminished self-confidence, and even sexual insecurity. Some people turn to crime as a way of solving the problem.

Even those people whose nominal incomes keep up with inflation often feel oppressed by rising prices. People feel that they deserve any increases in wages they receive. When they later discover that their higher (nominal) wages don't buy any additional goods, they feel cheated. They feel worse off, even though they haven't suffered any actual loss of real income.

This phenomenon is called **money illusion**. People suffering from money illusion are forever reminding society that they used to pay only $ 1 to see a movie or $8 for a textbook. What they forget is that nominal incomes were also a lot lower in the "good old days" then they are today.

Although redistributions of income and wealth are the primary consequences of inflation, inflation has macroeconomic effects as well. Inflation can alter the rate and mix of output by changing consumption, work, saving, investment, and trade behavior.

One of the most immediate consequences of inflation is **uncertainty**. When the average price level is changing significantly in either direction, economic decisions become more difficult. As the accompanying cartoon suggests, even something as simple as ordering a restaurant meal is more difficult if menu prices are changing (as they did during Germany's 1923 runaway inflation). Longer-term decisions are even more difficult. Should you commit yourself to four years of college, for example, if you aren't certain that you or your parents will be able to afford the full costs? In a period of stable prices you can be fairly certain of what a college education will cost. But if prices are rising, you can no longer be sure how large the bill will be. Under such circumstances, some individuals may decide not to enter college rather than risk the possibility of being driven out later by rising costs.

Price uncertainties affect production decision as well. Imagine a firm that's considering building a new factory. Typically, the construction of a factory takes two years or more, including planning, site selection, and actual construction. If construction costs change rapidly, the firm may find that it's unable to complete the factory or to operate it profitably. Confronted with the added uncertainty, the firm may decide not to build a new plant in the first place.

When market participants become less certain about the future, the economy is likely to suffer in the end. In general, people shorten their time horizons in the face of inflation uncertainties. If consumers and producers postpone or cancel their expenditure plans, the demand for goods and services will fall. Eventually our production of goods and services will fall as well, and we'll end up somewhere inside our production possibilities curve, with increased unemployment.

The effect of rising price levels on time horizons was dramatically illustrated during Germany's hyperinflation of the early 1920s. With prices doubling every week, German workers couldn't afford to wait until the end of the week to do their shopping. Instead, they were paid twice daily and given brief "shopping breaks" to make their essential purchases. In this case, the rate of expenditure on goods and services actually increased as a result of inflation, but the rate of production fell. The same kind of frenzy occurred in China during 1948 and 1949. The Nationalist Chinese Yuan declined precipitously in value, and market participants rushed to spend their incomes as fast as they could. No one saved income or even tried to.

Hyperinflation also crippled the Russian economy during the period 1990-92. Prices rose by 200 percent in 1991 and by another 1,000 percent in 1992. These price increases rendered the Russian ruble nearly worthless. No one wanted to hold rubles or trade for them. Farmers preferred to hold potatoes rather then sell them. Producers of shoes and clothes likewise decided to hold rather than sell their products. The resulting contraction in supply caused a severe decline in Russian output.

Inflation threatens not only to reduce the level of economic activity but to change its very nature. If you really expect prices to rise, it makes sense to buy goods and resources now for resale later. If prices rise fast enough, you can make a handsome profit. These are the kinds of thoughts that motivate people to buy houses, precious metals, commodities and other assets. But such speculation, if carried too far, can detract from the production process. If speculative profits become too easy, few people will engage in production; instead, everyone will be buying and selling existing goods. People may even be encouraged to withhold resources from the production process, hoping to sell them later at higher prices, which is what Russian farmers were doing in 1991 when they withheld potatoes from the market. As such behavior becomes widespread, production declines and unemployment rises.

Another reason that savings, investment, and work effort decline when prices rise is that taxes go up, too. Federal income tax rates are progressive; that is, tax rates are higher for larger incomes. The intent of these progressive rates is to redistribute income from rich to poor. However, inflation tends to increase everyone's income. In the process, people are pushed into higher tax brackets and confront higher tax rates. The process is referred to as bracket creep. In recent years, bracket creep has been limited by the inflation indexing of personal income tax rates and a reduction in the number of tax brackets. However, Social Security payroll taxes and most state and local taxes aren't indexed.

The CPI is often used to adjust consumers' income payment (for example, Social Security) to adjust income eligibility levels for government assistance and to automatically provide cost-of-living wage adjustments to millions of American workers. As a result of statutory action the CPI affects the income of about 80 million persons: the 51.6 million Social Security beneficiaries, about 21.3 million food stamp recipients, and about 4.6 million military and Federal Civil Service retirees and survivors. Changes in the CPI also affect the cost of lunches for 28.4 million children who eat lunch at school, while collective bargaining agreements that tie wages to the CPI cover over 2 million workers. Another example of how dollar values may be adjusted is the use of the CPI to adjust the Federal income tax structure. These adjustments prevent inflation-induced increases in tax rates, an effect called bracket creep. (stats. bls. gov)

Although the public sector still reaps some gain from inflation, inflation stress tends to create a political backlash. Voters are quick to blame the government for inflation. If the administration doesn't put a stop to inflation, the voters will turn to someone who promises to do so.

Ironically, a falling price level—a deflation—might not make people happy either. In fact, a falling price level can do the same kind of harm as a rising price level. When prices are falling, people on fixed incomes and long-term contracts gain more real income. Lenders win and creditors lose. People who hold cash or bonds win, homeowners and stamp collectors lose. A deflation simply reverses the kinds of redistributions caused by inflation.

A falling price level also has similar macro consequences. Time horizons get shorter. Businesses are more reluctant to borrow money or to invest. People lose confidence in themselves and public institutions when declining price levels deflate their incomes and assets.

Frederic S. Mishkin, an Alfred Lerner Professor of Banking and a former governor of the Federal Reserve Bank made the following remarks on inflation and the need for price stability—"There is now a broad consensus among policymakers, academic economists, and the general public in support of the principle that maintaining a low and stable inflation rate provides lasting benefits to the economy. In particular, low and predictable inflation promotes social welfare by simplifying the savings and retirement planning of individual households and by facilitating firms' production and investment decisions. Furthermore, an environment of overall price stability contributes to economic efficiency by reducing the variability of relative prices and by minimizing the distortions that arise because the tax system is not completely indexed to inflation.

Price stability also has important benefits in terms of equity. For example, an elevated inflation rate typically increases poverty because the poorest members of society do not have access to the sorts of financial instruments that would help protect them against inflation. By the way, these are not just theoretical arguments: The experience of the United States in the 1970s, and that of many other economies across a wide range of times and circumstances, demonstrates that high and unstable inflation generally detracts from the standard of living, hinders the process of capital formation and economic growth, and in some countries has even led to political and social instability. Such episodes also show that a full recovery from the adverse effects of severe inflation can take many years.

A central element in successful monetary policy is a strong commitment to a nominal anchor, that is, the use of monetary policy actions and statements to maintain low and stable inflation. During the 1980s and 1990s, the Federal Reserve succeeded in bringing inflation down from double-digit levels to the average rate of about 2 percent that has prevailed over the past decade. Moreover, when some measures of inflation were close to 1 percent in 2003, the Federal Open Market Committee's official statements specifically noted that any further substantial decline in inflation would be unwelcome, mainly because of the risk that a falling price level (which has not occurred since the Great Depression) could cause a significant disruption to economic activity and employment.

In recent years, the Federal Reserve has been quite successful in maintaining a nominal anchor. Not only has the inflation rate remained within a reasonably narrow range, but also inflation expectations as measured by spreads between inflation-indexed and non-inflation-indexed Treasury securities and by surveys of professional forecasters and the general public, has also been well anchored.

Maintaining price stability is also essential for achieving the other element of the dual mandate, namely, maximum sustainable employment. First, as I have already emphasized, a low and predictable inflation rate plays a crucial role in facilitating long-term growth in employment and labor productivity. Second, although the economy will inevitably be buffeted by various shocks, in the majority of circumstances the appropriate monetary policy response to stabilize inflation also helps to stabilize employment and output fluctuations around their maximum sustainable levels. In other words, the two elements of the dual mandate are usually complementary.

To see how a commitment to price stability leads to appropriate policy actions to stabilize employment and output fluctuations, we need to understand that there are two key determinants of inflations: inflation expectations and the amount of slack in the economy. Maintaining a nominal anchor helps stabilize inflation expectations, which in turn means that rises or falls in inflation tends to be highly correlated with economic slack. Thus, stabilizing inflation also helps to stabilize economic activity around sustainable levels.

To see further how this process would work, consider a negative shock to aggregate demand (such as a decline in consumer confidence) that causes households to cut spending. The drop in demand leads, in turn, to a decline in actual output relative to its potential, that is, the level of output that the economy can produce at the maximum sustainable level of employment. As a result, future inflation will fall below levels consistent with price stability, and the central bank will pursue an expansionary policy to keep inflation from falling. The expansionary policy will then result in an increase in demand that raises output back up to potential output in order to return inflation to a level consistent with price stability.

For example, during the last recession the Federal Reserve reduced its target for the federal funds rate a total of 5-1/2 percentage points, and this stimulus not only contributed to economic recovery but also helped avoid an unwelcome further decline in inflation. In other cases, a tightening of the stance of monetary policy is needed to prevent an "overheating" of economic activity, thereby avoiding a boom-bust cycle in the level of employment as well as an undesirable upward spurt of inflation.

A strong commitment to price stability helps reduce fluctuations in employment and output in other ways. First, when inflation expectations are well anchored, a central bank will not have to worry that expansionary policy to counter a negative demand shock will lead to sharp rise in expected inflation-a-so-called inflation scare-that will then push up actual inflation in the future. Thus, a strong commitment to a normal anchor enables a central bank to be more aggressive in the face of negative shocks and therefore to prevent rapid declines in employment or output.

Moreover, with a strong commitment to a nominal anchor, supply shocks to inflation, such as a rise in relative energy prices, are likely to have only a temporary effect on inflation. This result is exactly what we have seen in the United States. Because people are confident that the Fed will not allow inflation to remain high, the recent sharp run-up in oil prices did not lead to a sustained rise in longer-run inflation expectations. As a result, inflation rose temporarily but has now been falling back again. When inflation expectations are well-anchored, the occurrence of an adverse aggregate supply shock does not necessarily mean that the central bank must raise interest rates aggressively in order to keep inflation under control, and hence the commitment to price stability can help avoid imposing unnecessary harm on the economy and on the workers who are most vulnerable to a weakening of economic activity.

Now that we see the benefits of maintaining a commitment to a nominal anchor, one might naturally think that there would also be benefits to establishing a similar sort of anchor for the maximum level of employment. But that thought would be incorrect.

In particular, although the Federal Reserve can determine and achieve the long-run average rate of inflation in keeping with its mandate of price stability, the level of maximum sustainable employment is not something that can be chosen by the Federal Reserve because no central bank can control the level of real economic activity or employment over the longer run. As I've already emphasized, monetary policy can certainly help improve the maximum sustainable employment of the economy by maintaining low and predictable inflation. But any attempt to use stimulative monetary policy to maintain employment above its long-run sustainable level will inevitably lead to an upward spiral of inflation and therefore will actually undermine the productive capacity of the economy, with severe adverse consequences for household income and employment.

Indeed, the level of maximum sustainable employment is primarily driven by the fundamental structure of the economy, including factors such as demographics, people's preferences, the efficiency of labor markets, the characteristics of the tax code, and so forth. And many policies outside the control of the Fed can have a significant effect on the efficiency of the economy and hence on the maximum sustainable level of employment." (Mishkin, 2007)

CHAPTER THREE

WHAT IS INFLATION TARGETING

There is a large and growing literature on inflation targeting that includes much disagreement about what it is and whether it is a good monetary policy. The conference volume titled "The Inflation Targeting Debate" edited by Ben S. Bernanke and Michael Woodford includes an impressive compilation of papers detailing the state of this debate.

Regardless of the inflation target model that a central bank chooses, inflation targeting is a monetary policy in which a Central Bank estimates and makes public, a projected or "target" inflation rate and then attempts to steer actual inflation towards the target through the use of interest rate changes and other monetary tools that can be used to affect money supply.

If inflation appears to be above target, for example, the Central Bank is likely to influence interest rate upward which has the effect over time to "cool off" the economy to bring Inflation down. Conversely, if inflation appears to be below target, the Central Bank is likely to influence interest rates downwards, which over time accelerates the economy, which in turn spurs inflation.

Bernanke and Mishkin in their contribution to the subject did regard inflation targeting as a "framework, not a rule". They view it as a monetary policy framework that provides a clearly defined nominal target, a coherent approach to decision making, the flexibility to respond to unanticipated shocks, and a strategy for communicating with the public and financial markets. (Bernanke & Woodford, 2003)

OTHER TECHNIQUES OF CONTROLLING INFLATION

There are varied remedies suggested by economists of different persuasions.

The monetarist or neo-classicals emphasize increasing interest rates, by reducing the money supply through monetary policy to fight inflation. Keynesians and neo-Keynesians emphasize reducing demand in general, often through fiscal policy, using increased taxation or reduced government spending to reduce demand as well as by using monetary policy.

The supply side economists argue the importance of lowering marginal tax rates, which they say stimulates **aggregate supply** by encouraging suppliers to produce more, and individuals to earn more as opposed to stimulating aggregate demand for goods and services by consumers and business so that **there will not be "too much money changing too few goods"**, the opposite will prevail to bring inflation down. The supply side approach was "Reaganomics" (Pres. Regan Economic Policies) solution to the stagflation (double digit inflation accompanied by stagnant growth) that existed before his time in the early 1980's. Most supply-siders also advocated fighting inflation by fixing the value of the nation's currency unit to a fixed amount of gold bullion, which is also a measure subscribed to by the Austrian School. The Austrians also believe in fighting inflation with money supply and real rate of interest.

Wage and Price controls have been introduced by various economies at different periods. Wage and Price controls have been successful in wartime environment in combination with rationing. The benefits of price control in other times is said to be mixed. Ghana applied price controls in the early 1970's, while it was welcomed by the lower economic class, it was resented by traders and captains of commerce which resulted in hoarding, acute shortages, further misery and black marketing, therefore inflation was really not fought but rather exacerbated.

Another notable failure was the 1972 ninety day wage and price control measures imposed by President Nixon in the United States.

Price controls are unpopular among economists, they are deemed effective when coupled with polices designed to reduce the underlying cause of inflation during a wage and price control regime, especially in times of war.

Many developed nations set prices extensively, especially for basic commodities as gasoline. The usual economic analysis is that goods under priced are over consumed, and that the distortions that occur will force adjustments in supply. For example, if the official price of bread is too low, there will be too little bread at official prices.

Temporary controls may complement recession as a way to fight inflation: the controls make the recession more efficient as a way to fight inflation (reducing the acceleration of unemployment), while the recession prevents the kinds of distortions that controls cause when demand is high. However, in general the advice of economists is not to impose price controls, but to liberalize prices, assuming that the economy will adjust, abandoning unprofitable economic activity. The lower activity will place fewer demands on whatever commodities were driving inflation, whether labor or other resources, and inflation will fall with total economic output. This often produces a severe recession, as productive capacity is reallocated, and is thus often very unpopular with the people whose livelihoods are destroyed. (Reisman, 1990)

Central Banks have used various monetary polices as a means to constrain inflation. Some of the polices are Inflation Targeting, Price Level Targeting, Monetary Aggregates, Fixed Exchange Rate, Gold Standard (now extinct) and Mixed Policy. The distinctions between the various types of monetary policy lies primarily with the market variable that open market are used to target. (Mishkin, 1995).

The tools mostly used to pursue these polices are **open market operations**, **reserve requirements** and **last resort Lending rate**. In practice all the monetary polices attempt to modify the amount of base currency (MO) in circulation through open market operations.

PRICE LEVEL TARGETING

Price level targeting is similar to inflation targeting except that CPI growth in one year is offset in subsequent years such that over time the price level on aggregate does not move.

Something like price level targeting was tried in the 1930s by Sweden, and seems to have contributed to the relatively good performance of the Swedish economy during the Great Depression. As of 2004, no country operates monetary policy based on a price level target.

MONETARY AGGREGATES

This policy usually intends a constant growth of a particular monetary aggregate, usually M2.If the targeted aggregate exceeds target it indicates inflation and then a correction is effected. This policy was popular in the 1980's. In the USA this approach to a monetary policy was discontinued with the selection of Alan Greenspan as Fed Chairman. This approach is also sometimes called monetarism.

Whilst most monetary policy focuses on a price signal of one form or another this approach is focused on monetary quantities.

FIXED EXCHANGE RATE

This policy is based on maintaining a fixed exchange rate with a foreign currency. Currency is bought and sold by the central bank on a daily basis to achieve the target exchange rate. This policy somewhat abdicates responsibility for monetary policy to a foreign government, but it is said to have the ability of limiting the amount of Paper Currency a government can issue for domestic spending.

This type of policy was used by China. The Chinese Yuan was managed such that its exchange rate with the United States dollar was fixed.

GOLD STANDARD

GOLD STANDARD monetary system pegs or fixes the value of a nation's currency unit to fixed amount of gold bullion. Paper currency in such systems is convertible freely into gold. The gold standard was introduced in Great Britain in 1821 and was the basis for the U.S monetary system from the 1870s to 1971, when the U.S Treasury Department announced it would no longer back the U.S dollar, for foreign exchange purposes, with its gold reserves. (The Gold Act of 1934 abolished the right U.S citizens to exchange paper currency for gold). The gold standard insures a fixed rate of exchange in international trade, while limiting the amount of paper currency central government can issue for domestic spending. Its main drawback is that it hinders the ability of a government to control the supply of money and it makes it very difficult for a country to isolate itself from depressions or inflation in the economies of its major trading partners. A country experiencing a large BALNCE OF PAYMENT deficit may thus find it impossible to properly address the situation without coming off the gold standard. It is said to be simple and transparent.

Gold standard is not used by any Central Bank today. It was used prior to 1971. It was dislodged by the Smithsonian agreement in 1972. It is however being advocated by some for its return.

MIXED POLICY

In practice a mixed policy approach is most like "inflation targeting". However some consideration is also given to other goals such as economic growth, unemployment and asset bubbles. The U.S Federal Reserve uses a mixed Policy called dual mandate-maximum employment and price stability. Under the Full Employment and Balance Growth Act, the Federal Reserve Board must keep inflation under 3 percent, annually.

RESERVE REQUIREMENTS

This is the situation where portions of deposits depository institutions are required to maintain as LEGAL RESERVES for the protection of depositors. Reserve requirements also provide one of the **monetary adjustment tools** the Federal

Reserve System employs to regulate the supply of credit in the banking system. By raising or lowering the amount of required reserves, the Federal Reserve can either stimulate or tighten available bank credit, and the ability of banks to lend-known as fractional reserve banking.

DISCOUNT WINDOW OR LAST RESORT LENDING

Many central banks or finance ministries have the authority to lend funds to financial institutions within their country. The borrowed funds represent an expansion in the monetary base. By calling in existing loans or extending new loans, the monetary authority can directly change the size of the money supply to affect or neutralize inflation. In the United States, Discount rates can be set to influence the federal funds rate (inter-bank rate).

INTEREST RATE REGULATIONS

In some countries, the monetary authority may be able to regulate specific interest rates on loans, saving accounts or other financial assets. By raising the interest rate, a monetary authority can contract the money supply, because higher interest rates encourage savings and discourage lending or borrowing, to control money supply. Such was the case in the U.S. before Depository Institution Deregulation and Monetary Control Act of 1980.

CURRENCY BOARD

A currency board is a monetary authority, which is required to maintain an exchange rate with a foreign currency. This policy objective requires the conventional objectives of central bank to be subordinated to the exchange rate target.

The currency board in question will no longer issue fiat money but instead will only issue a set number of units of local currency for each unit of foreign currency it has in its vault.

The surplus on the balance of payments of that country is reflected by higher deposits local banks hold at the central bank as well as (initially) higher deposits of the (net) exporting firms at their local banks. The growth of the domestic money supply can now be coupled to the additional deposits of the banks at the central bank that equals additional hard foreign exchange reserves in the hands of the central bank. The virtue of this system is currency stability. The drawbacks are that the country no longer has the ability to set monetary policy according to other domestic considerations, and that the fixed exchange rate will, to a large extent, also fix a country's terms of trade, irrespective of economic differences between it and its trading partners.

Hong Kong operates a currency board, as does Bulgaria. Estonia established a currency board pegged to the Deutschmark in 1992 after gaining independence, and this policy is seen as a mainstay of that country's subsequent economic success. Argentina abandoned its currency board in January 2002 after a severe recession. This emphasized the fact that currency boards are not irrevocable, and hence may be abandoned in the face of speculation by foreign exchange traders.

Currency boards have advantages for small, open economies, which would find independent monetary policy difficult to sustain. They can also form a credible commitment to low inflation.

A gold standard is a special case of a currency board where the value of the national currency is linked to the value of gold instead of a foreign currency.

EVOLUTION AND HISTORY OF INFLATION TARGETING

Over the last thirty years, a consensus has been emerging in the study of monetary economics that activist monetary policy to stimulate output and reduce unemployment beyond their sustainable levels leads to higher inflation but not to persistently lower unemployment or higher output. Thus the commitment to price stability as the primary goal for monetary policy has been spreading throughout the world.

According to Mishkin and Posen (1997) this consensus has been influenced by four intellectual developments:

"The first intellectual development challenging the use of an activist monetary policy to stimulate output and reduce unemployment is the finding, most forcefully articulated by Milton Friedman, that the effects of monetary policy have long variable lags. The uncertainty of the timing and the size of monetary policy effects makes it very possible that attempts to stabilize outputs fluctuations may not have the desired results. In fact, activist monetary policy can at times be counterproductive, pushing the economy further away from equilibrium, particularly when the stance of monetary policy is unclear to the public and even to policymakers. This lack of clarity makes it very difficult for policymakers to successfully design policy to reduce output unemployment fluctuations.

The second development is the general acceptance of the view that there is no long-run trade-off between inflation and unemployment. The so-called Phillips curve relationship illustrates the empirical regularity that a lower unemployment rate or higher output can be achieved in the short run by expansionary policy that leads to higher inflation. As prices rise, households and businesses spend and produce more because they temporarily believe themselves to be better off as a result of higher nominal wages and profits, or because they perceive that demand in the economy is growing. In the long run, however, the rise in output or decline in unemployment cannot persist because of capacity constraints in the economy, while the rise in inflation can persist because it becomes embedded in price expectations. Thus, over the long-run, attempts to exploit the short-run Phillips curve trade-off only result in higher inflation, but have no benefit for real economic activity.

The third intellectual development calling into question the use of an activist monetary policy to stimulate output and reduce unemployment is commonly referred to as the time-inconsistency problem of monetary policy. The time-inconsistency problem stems from the view that wage—and price-setting behavior is influenced by expectations of future monetary policy. A frequent starting point for discussing policy decisions is to assume that private sector expectations are given at the time policy is made. With expectations fixed, policymakers know they can boost economic output (or lower unemployment) by pursuing monetary policy that is more expansionary than expected. As a result, policymakers who have a stronger interest in output than in inflation performance will try to produce monetary policy that is more expansionary than expected. However, because workers and firms make decisions about wages and prices on the basis of their expectations about policy, they will recognize the policy makers' incentive for expansionary monetary policy and so will raise their expectations of inflation. As a result, wages and prices will rise.

The outcome, in these time-inconsistency models, is that policymakers are actually unable to fool workers and firms, so that on average output will not be higher under such a strategy; unfortunately, however, inflation will be.

The time-inconsistency problem suggests that a central bank pursuing output goals may end up with a bias to high inflation with no gains in output. Consequently, even though the central bank believes itself to be operating in an optimal manner, it ends up with a suboptimal outcome.

MaCallum (1995) points out that the time inconsistency problem by itself does not imply that a central bank will pursue expansionary monetary policy that leads to inflation. Simply by recognizing the problem that forward looking expectations in the wage-and price-setting process create for a strategy of pursuing unexpectedly expansionary monetary policy, central banks can decide not to play that game. Nonetheless, the time—inconsistency literature points out both why there will be pressures on central banks to pursue overly expansionary monetary policy and why central bank whose commitment to price stability is in doubt can experience higher inflation.

A fourth intellectual development challenging the use of an activist monetary policy to stimulate output and reduce unemployment unduly is the recognition that price stability promotes an economic system that functions more efficiently and so raises living standards. If price stability does not persist—that is, inflation occurs—the society suffers several economic costs. While these costs tend to be much larger in economies with high rates of inflation (usually defined to be inflation in excess of 30 percent a year), recent work shows that substantial costs arise even at low rates of inflation.

COSTS OF INFLATION

The cost that first-received the attention of economists is the so-called shoe leather cost of Inflation—the cost of economizing on the use of non-interest-bearing money (see Baily 1956). The history of prewar central Europe make us all too familiar with the difficulties of requiring vast and ever-rising quantities of cash to conduct daily transactions.

Unfortunately, hyperinflations have occurred in emerging market countries within the last decade as well. Given conventional estimates of the interest elasticity of money and the real interest rate when inflation is zero, this cost is quite low for inflation rates less than 10 percent, remaining below 0.10 percent of GDP. Only when inflation rises to above 100 percent do these costs become appreciable, climbing above 1 percent of GDP (Fischer 1981).

Another cost of inflation related to the additional need for transactions is the inflation related to the additional need for transactions is the overinvestment in the financial sector induced by inflation. At the margin, opportunities to make profits by acting as a middleman on normal transactions, rather than investing in productive activities, increase with instability in prices. A number of estimates put the rise in the financial sector share of GDP on the order of 1 percentage point for every 10 percentage points of inflation up of an inflation rate of 100 percent (English 1996). The transfer of resources out of productive uses else-where in the economy can be as large as a few percentage points of GDP and can even be seen at relatively low or moderate rates of inflation.

The difficulties caused by inflation can also extend to decisions about future expenditures. Higher inflation increase uncertainty about both relative prices and the future price level, which makes it harder to arrive at the appropriate production decisions. For example, in labor markets, Groshen and Schweitzer (1996) calculate that the loss of output due to inflation of 10 percent (compared with a level of 2 percent) is 2 percent of GDP. More broadly, the uncertainty about relative prices induced by inflation can distort the entire pricing mechanism. Under inflationary conditions, the risk premia demanded on savings and the frequency with which prices are changed increase. Inflation also alters the relative attractiveness of real versus nominal assets for investment and short-term versus-long-term contracting.

The most obvious costs of inflation at low to moderate levels seems to come from the interaction of the tax system with inflation. Because tax systems are rarely indexed for inflation, an increase in inflation substantially raises the cost of capital, causing investment to drop below its optimal level. In addition, higher taxation, which results from inflation, causes a misallocation of capital to different sectors, which in turn distorts the labor supply and leads to inappropriate corporate financing decisions. Fischer (1997) calculates that the social costs from the tax-related distortions of inflation amount to 2 to 3 percent of GDP at an inflation rate of 10 percent. In a recent paper, Feldstein (1996) estimates this cost to be even higher: he calculates the cost of an inflation rate of 2 percent rather than zero to be 1 percent of GDP.

The cost of inflation outlined here decrease the level of resources productively employed in an economy, and thereby the base from which the economy can grow. Mounting evidence from econometric studies shows that, at high levels, inflation also decreases the rate of growth of economies. While time series studies of individual countries over long periods and cross-national comparisons of growth rates are not in total agreement, the consensus is that, on average, a 1 percent rise in inflation can cost an economy 0.1 to 0.5 percentage points in its rate of growth (Fischer 1993). This result varies greatly with the level of inflation—the effects are usually thought to be much greater at higher levels. However, a recent study has presented evidence that the inflation variability usually associated with higher inflation has a significant negative effect on growth even at low levels of inflation, in addition to and distinct from the direct effect of inflation itself?

The four lines of argument outlined here lead the vast majority of central bankers and academic monetary economists to the view that price stability should be the primary long-term goal for policy. Furthermore, to avoid the tendency to an inflationary bias produced by the time-inconsistency problem (or uncertainty about monetary policy goals more generally), monetary policy strategy often relies upon a nominal anchor to serve as a target that ties the central bank's hands so it cannot pursue (or be pressured into pursing) a strategy of raising output with unexpectedly expansionary monetary policy.

As a result of the above Central Bankers had practiced intermediate targeting one time or another that involved pre-announced exchange rate rule or targets for specific monetary aggregates. Under the exchange rate rule monetary policy is severely limited because it is directed only at exchange rate, thus constraining the ability of central bank to respond to domestic or external shocks. Not only is the country unable to use monetary policy to respond to domestic shocks, but it is also vulnerable to shocks emanating from the country to which its currency is pegged. Furthermore, in the current environment of open, global capital markets, fixed exchange rate regimes are subject to breakdowns that may entail sharp changes in exchanges rates. Such developments can be very disruptive to a country's economy, as recent events in Mexico have demonstrated. Defending the domestic currency when it is under pressure may require substantial increases in interest rates that directly cause a contraction in consumer and investment spending, and the contraction in turn may lead to a recession. In addition, as pointed out in Mishkin (1996), a sharp depreciation of the domestic currency can produce a full-scale banking and financial crisis that can trip a country's economy into a severe depression. With monetary aggregate targeting, a Central Bank sets a target growth path for a monetary aggregate such as the monetary base or M1, M2 or M3. If velocity is either relatively constant or predictably, a growth target of a monetary aggregate can keep nominal income on a steady growth path that lead to long-term price stability. In such an environment, choosing a monetary aggregate as a nominal anchor has several advantages. First, some monetary aggregates, the narrower the better, can be controlled both quickly and easily by the central bank. Second, monetary aggregates can be measured quite accurately with short lags (in the case of the United States, for example, measures of the monetary aggregates appear within two weeks. Third, as pointed out in Bernanke and Mishkin (1992), because an aggregate is known so quickly, using it as a nominal anchor greatly increase the transparency of monetary policy, which can have important benefits. A monetary aggregate sends almost immediate signals to both the public and the markets about the stance of monetary policy and the intentions of policymakers, thereby helping to fix inflation expectations. In addition, the transparency of a monetary aggregate target makes the central bank more accountable to the public to keep inflation low, which can help reduce pressures on the Central bank to pursue expansionary monetary policy.

Although the targeting of monetary aggregates has many important advantages in principle, in practice these advantages come about only if the monetary aggregates have a highly predictable relationship with nominal income. Unfortunately, in many countries, velocity fluctuations have been so large and frequent in the last twenty years that the relationships between monetary aggregates and goal variables have broken down. Some observers have gone so far as to argue that attempts to exploit these relationships have been a cause of their breakdown. As a result, the use of monetary aggregate targets as a nominal anchor has become highly problematic, and many countries that adopted monetary targets in the 1970s abandoned them in the 1980s. Not surprisingly, many policymakers have been looking for a alternative nominal anchors.

An inflation target (or its variant, a price-level target) clearly provides a nominal anchor for the path of the price level, and, like a fixed exchange rate anchor, has the important advantage of being easily understood by the public. The resulting transparency increases the potential for promoting low inflation expectations, which helps to produce a desirable inflation outcome. Also, like a fixed exchange rate or a monetary targeting strategy, inflation targeting reduces the pressure on the monetary authorities to pursue short-run output gains that would lead to the time-inconsistency problem. Inflation-targeting strategy also avoids several of the problems arising from monetary targeting or fixed exchange **rate** strategies. For example, in contrast to a fixed exchange rate system, inflation targeting can preserve a country's independent monetary policy so that the monetary authorities can cope with domestic shocks and help insulate the domestic economy from foreign shocks. In addition, inflation targeting can avoid the problem presented by velocity shocks because it eliminates the need to focus on the link between a monetary aggregate and nominal income; instead, all relevant information may be brought to bear in forecasting inflation and choosing a policy response to achieve a desirable inflation outcome."

While most developing countries adopted some form of exchange rate targeting following the breakdown of the Bretton Woods arrangement in the mid-1970s, two-thirds of these countries currently follow more flexible exchange rate arrangements. Nevertheless, a number of developing and transition countries continue to maintain fixed or quasi-fixed exchange rates, and some previously high-inflation economies (for example, Argentina since 1991 and Brazil during 1994-98) have effectively used pegged rates to reduce inflation quickly. However, with the growing integration of world capital markets over the past two decades and the increased volatility of capital flows since the 1992 European Monetary System (EMS) crisis, and especially after the more recent financial crises in Asia and Latin America, the conditions for maintaining a fixed exchange rate system have become much more demanding. As a consequence, developing and transition economies that still maintain a fixed exchange rate as a nominal anchor for monetary policy are coming under mounting pressure to move either toward flexible arrangements or to the other extreme of the spectrum, such as currency boards or full-fledged dollarization.

Industrial countries—with the notable exception of EMS members in their arrangements with each other—have traditionally favored more flexible exchange rate arrangements in the post—Bretton Woods' era, with the majority opting for some kind of monetary targeting regime. However, during the 1980s, countries experience with monetary targeting became unsatisfactory. As financial institutions developed money substitutes, the demand for money became increasingly unstable, and it became apparent that, although highly correlated in the long run, money and inflation were not sufficiently correlated in the short run. As a result, in the early 1990s, several Organization for Economic Cooperation and Development countries—first New, Zealand, then Canada, Israel, the United Kingdom, Australia, Finland, Spain, and Sweden—adopted explicit inflation targeting as a strategy for conducting monetary policy.

INFLATION TARGETING FRAMEWORK

Once a case (through mandate or policy) has been made for a Central Bank to implement Inflation Targeting, the respective Central Bank comes into the unsettled debate over inflation targeting.

The debate is on four basic categories: definition and measurement of the target, transparency, flexibility and timing. In theses categories one will be faced with questions about the appropriate choice of price index and numerical inflation target, whether policy should be conducted through rules or by discretion and whether inflation targeting is sufficient for the conduct of monetary policy.

DEFINITION AND MEASUREMENT OF THE TARGET

The phrase "inflation targeting" connotes a numerical value for the target. To set a target Central Banks must have explicit answers for the following questions:

What does price stability means in practice? Central Banks must come out with a quantitative statement as to what inflation rate is consistent with the pursuit of price stability in the next few years. Because of technology and innovation that brings out new products and consumers changing tastes, all inflation measures have a net positive bias. For example, measurement error for consumer price index (CPI) inflation in the United States has been estimated to be in the range of 0.5 to 2.0 percent at an annual rate (Shapiro and Wilcox 1996). Another factor to be taken into account in setting the target level of inflation is the asymmetric dangers from deflation. That is, through financial and other channels, the costs to the real economy from undershooting zero inflation outweigh the direct costs to the economy from overshooting zero inflation by a similar amount. These potential costs might warrant setting the inflation target a little above zero.

What inflation index should be targeted and who should measure it? A decision has to made what inflation target index is to be used and what agency to measure. The index series needs to be considered accurate, timely, and readily understandable by the public. The index may have to exclude from its definition individual price shocks to one-time shifts that do not affect trend inflation.

How should inflation targets be communicated with the public and the markets? This is the decision on how or the medium the central bank has to employ to communicate targets to the public and the markets. This way the public and the markets know about the stance and intentions of monetary policy. A number of institutional arrangements, published materials, testimony and speeches can help in this communication process and can emphasize the forward-looking nature of monetary policy. The institutional arrangement for communication fosters transparency. Also clear, regular explanations of monetary policy by central banks can build public support for and understanding of the pursuit of price stability. Effective communication on the need for low inflation environment has the propensity to influence fiscal discipline.

How central banks should be held accountable for target performance? A major feature for the inflation targeting framework is the institutional arrangement for accounting. In addition to what the legal mandates provide, the central bank may also add on any more measures that they can be measured by. All in a bid to earn credibility.

What deviations from the inflation target should be allowed in response to shocks? Because both policymakers and the public care about output fluctuations, and the public care about output fluctuations, and the ultimate reason for price stability is to support a healthy real economy, an inflation-targeting regime may need escape clauses or some flexibility built into the target definition to deal with supply and other types of shocks.(Mishkin & Posen 1997).

Should the target be a point or a range? Due to shocks like negative supply shocks, natural disasters and even terrorism to the inflation process and uncertainty about the effects of monetary policy, inflation outcomes can have a high degree of uncertainty even with the best monetary policy settings therefore a decision will have to be made whether target should be point or range and if it is point the tolerance for deviation.

Should inflation targets be varied over time? Varying inflation targets over time is another tool to increase the flexibility of the inflation-targeting regime so that it can cope with supply and other types of shocks including terrorism to an economy, but ground rules must be preset for the need to vary. It usually must be initiated by the government or the mandator as in the case of New Zealand. (Discussed later).

What is the appropriate time horizon for an inflation target? Due to the fact that monetary policy affects inflation with usually long lags, monetary policy cannot achieve a specific inflation target immediately, but instead achieves its goal over time. Also, economic shocks can occur in the intervening period between policy and effect therefore monetary policymakers must decide what time horizon is appropriate for meeting the inflation target.

When is the best time to start implementing inflation targets? To establish credibility for inflation-targeting regime, it may be important to have some initial successes in achieving the inflation targets. This suggests that certain periods may be better than others to introduce inflation targets. Furthermore, obtaining political support for the commitment to price stability underlying inflation-targeting regime may be easier at certain times than at others, so choosing the correct time to implement inflation targeting may be an important element in its success or failure. (Mishkin & Posen 1997)

MODELS OF INFLATION TARGETING

All the Inflation Targeting regimes are ordered by their mandate to meet an arbitrary target either set by an Act or set by the Minister of Finance in conjunction with the governor of the respective Central Bank. The U.S Federal Reserve Bank, although not an 'explicit' but an 'implicit inflation targeting regime is said to use the Taylor rule frequently to come up with the federal funds rate that it targets to regulate money supply. The following is the Taylor rate:

$$i_t = \pi_t + r^*_t + a^*_\pi (\pi_t - \pi_t^*) + a_y (y_t - \bar{y}_t)$$

Where i_t is the target federal funds rate, π_t is the rate of inflation as measured by the GDP deflator, π_t^* is the desired rate of inflation, r^*_t is the assumed equilibrium real interest rate, y_t is the logarithm of real GDP, and Yt is the logarithm of potential output, as determined by a linear trend (Taylor, 1993).

The rule "recommends" a relatively high interest rate (that is, a "tight" monetary policy) when inflation is above its target or when the economy is above its full employment level, and a relatively low interest rate ("easy" monetary policy) in the opposite situation. Sometimes these goals are in conflict:

inflation may be above its target while the economy is below full employment (such as in the case of stagflation). In such situations, the rule provides guidance to policy makers on how to balance these competing considerations in setting an appropriate level for the interest rate.

Although the Fed does not explicitly follow the rule, analysis shows that the rule does a fairly accurate job of describing how monetary policy actually has been conducted during the past decade under Alan Greenspan. This fact has been cited by many economists inside and outside of the Fed as a reason that inflation has remained under control and that the economy has been relatively stable in the US over the past ten years.

Explicit inflation targeting Central Banks must set their monetary policy instruments-typically the influence of cash-rate or inter-bank lending rate (federal funds rate in the U.S.) rates, through open market operations to meet the inflation target set by their mandate or remit. In this sense inflation targeting has been described as a "framework for conducting monetary policy under constrained discretion "(Mishkin, Posen 1997)

It relies on rules, committing the Central Bank to policy consistency while at the same time it leaves the Central Bank the discretion to decide how to deploy its instruments to meet the Target and some flexibility to deal with unforeseen domestic and external shocks. Included in the rules or frameworks is the need to communicate to the public at large and instituting measures of accountability.

Constrained discretion attempts to strike a balance between the inflexibility of strict policy rules and the potential lack of discipline inherent in unfettered policymaker discretion. Under constrained discretion, the central bank is free to do its best to stabilize output and employment in the face of short-run disturbances, with the appropriate caution born of our imperfect knowledge of the economy and of the effects of policy (this is the "discretion" part of constrained discretion).However, a crucial proviso is that, in conducting stabilization policy, the central bank must also maintain a strong commitment to keeping inflation—and, hence, public expectations of inflation—firmly under control (the constrained" part of constrained discretion). Because monetary policy, influences inflation with a lag, keeping inflation under control may require the central bank to anticipate future movements in inflation and move preemptively. Hence constrained discretion is an inherently forward looking policy approach. (Bernanke, 2003).

A typical inflation-targeting central bank sets its instruments typically interest rates—today at a level that will bring inflation forecasts—for, say, inflation one or two years ahead—close to the inflation target at that future time. Inflation forecasts act as an intermediate target; the discrepancy between the forecast and the inflation target prompts policy choices to close the gap. The forward-looking approach is obviously desirable, given the long and variable lags between changes in the monetary instruments and their impact on the ultimate policy goal. By contrast, responding to past or current inflation would imply that policy is always reacting too late, increasing the likelihood of greater variability of inflation and output.

In practice, the central bank usually decides on the future course of monetary policy after assessing the information provided by a number of indicators, such as inflation forecasts provided by structural macroeconomic models, forecasts produced by more mechanical approaches—like vector autoregressive models—and surveys of a market based inflation expectations. The monetary authorities also consider developments in key monetary and financial variables, such as money and credit, the term structure of interest rates, asset prices, and labor market conditions. To the extent that more than one of these indicators suggests that future inflation is likely to exceed the target, the need to activate instruments becomes more evident. This process is called Inflation-Forecast Targeting. (Svensson and Woodford 2003)

Central Banks employ various econometric models to decide on the optimal inflation forecast.

The following are examples of Inflation-Targeting models:

1. **NEW ZEALAND:** In New Zealand, the first inflation targeting regime, the numerical target is set jointly by the Minister of Finance and the Governor of the Central Bank and is currently a range of 1 percent to 3 percent over the medium term, the widest of any of the ranges in inflation regimes. New Zealand is quite well-known for establishing performance contracts in the form of Policy Target Agreements between the Minister of Finance and the Central Bank Governor. This agreement is required by a 1989 Act that became effective in 1990. (*www.rbnz.govt.nz*).

2. **CANADA:** The Bank of Canada operates under the vaguest legal mandate among inflation targeting central banks. Its statute requires it to regulate "credit and currency in the best interests of the economic life of the nation" Despite the absence of a precise legal mandate, the details of the Bank's monetary policy objectives are reached by agreement between the Bank and the Department of Finance. This agreement has set price stability as the principal objective for monetary policy. Current target is set at 2 percentage points of CPI with plus or minus 1 percent tolerance. (www. bankofcanada.ca)

3. **AUSTRALIA:** The Reserve Bank of Australia has a mandate most closely resembling that of the U.S. though it is even broader and more open-ended. Their legislative mandate is "to promote stability of the currency of Australia; and foster economic prosperity and Welfare of the people of Australia." The explicit inflation target is between 2 and 3 percent CPI over the medium term. Although Australia is counted among inflation-targeting countries, it has a dual mandate rather than a hierarchical one. (www.rba.gov.au)

4. **UNITED KINGDOM:** The mandate in the United Kingdom is hierarchical. Article 11 of the Bank of England Act sets the objectives for monetary policy as "to maintain price stability" and "subject to that, to support the economic policy of Her Majesty's Government, including its objectives for growth and employment." The explicit target, set by the Chancellor of the Exchequer (the equivalent of the Minister of Finance in many countries or the Secretary of the Treasury in the United States), is currently 2 percent and the target is for retail prices excluding mortgage interest payments. The Governor of the Bank of England must write a letter to the Chancellor if inflation deviates by more than 1 percentage point from the target. *(www. bankofengland.com).*

5. **EUROPEAN CENTRAL BANK:** The ECB does not view itself as inflation-targeting Central Bank. However, the Maastricht Treaty-the equivalent of the statute establishing the objectives for a Central Bank—identifies price stability as the principal objective in the context of a hierarchical mandate. Article 105 of the Maastricht Treaty States that "the primary objectives of the European System of Central Bank (ESCB) shall

be to maintain price stability. Without prejudice to the objectives of price stability, the ESCB shall support the general economic policies in the community with a view to contributing to the objectives of the Community laid down in Article 2. "The objectives mentioned in Article 2 include "sustainable and non-inflationary growth," a "high level of employment," and "raising the standard of living" among member states. The ECB's Governing Council sets the explicit numerical inflation target. This is currently set with an explicit ceiling of 2 percent and an implicit lower bound of 0 percent. This is the case of a range rather than a point, with no preference stated for the midpoint. (Meyer, 2001). Table 1 depicts a chart of five inflation targeting model countries.

TABLE 1

INFLATION TARGETING FRAMEWORK OF FIVE COUNTRIES

Country	Date	Type of mandate	Setting	Transition period to reach final target	Time frame to correct deviations	Communication	Independence
New Zealand	Dec. 1989	Price stability	Range of 1-3% CPI over medium term	Yes	Not explicit	Quarterly monetary policy statement	No: Target set by agreement between government and bank
Canada	Feb. 1991	Multiple	2% points of CPI with± 1% tolerance	Yes	6-8 quarters	Quarterly monetary policy statement	No: Target set by government and bank
U. K.	Oct. 1992	Hierarchy with price stability first	2% points of CPI with± 1% tolerance	Yes	Not specific but required to set horizon each instance	Quarterly inflation report	No: Target set by government

Sweden	Jan 1993	Price Stability	2% points of annual CPI with ± 1% tolerance 1-2 years ahead	No	Yes 1-2 years	Quarterly inflation report	Yes
Australia	June 1993	Multiple	Rang of 2-3% CPI over medium term	No	No time frame	Quarterly statement on monetary policy	Yes

SOURCE: DOTSEY (2006)

ADVANTAGES OF INFLATION TARGETING

The advantages of Inflation Targeting are within the concept or framework of "Constrained Discretion." The advantages are maximized if inflation targeting is pursed under 'best practice'—independence of the Central Bank, 'flexible rather than 'strict' inflation practice and Transparency (explicit target and communication framework).

1. The target set in remits or mandates given to Central Banks effectively commits a Central Bank to a price level target path. This assures the Public of a commitment to a Low Inflation environment.
2. The Target in commitment makes a Central Bank accountable to its constituents. If a Central Bank misses its target, it will have to explain why the miss and if the explanation is not tenable, there could be change in the directors of the Central Bank. In New Zealand for example, the governor by statute can be dismissed if inflation performance is inadequate. Also, a Central Bank can build its reputation or credibility if it is able to meet its Target.
3. The communication part of the framework improves the clarity of monetary policy and therefore its effectiveness.

Other monetary policies can also be communicated but proponents of Inflation Targeting posit that it is easier for the general public to understand the explicit announcement of inflation targets than the growth rate of particular monetary aggregates.

4. Inflation Targeting in two parts, thus a policy framework of constrained discretion and communication strategy, attempts to focus expectations and explain the policy framework to the public. Together these two elements promote both price stability and well anchored inflation expectation. The latter in turn facilitates more effective stabilization of output and employment. Thus a well conceived and well executed strategy of Inflation Targeting can deliver good results with respect to output and employment as well as inflation. (Bernanke, 2003)

5. A long run inflation objective (or equivalently, a price-path target) works well because it gives consumers and firms a benchmark for wage and pricing decision over any relevant horizon. (Gavin 2003).

6. Inflation Targeting leads policy makers to debate, decide on and communicate the Inflation objective. Implemented well, a long-run inflation targeting strategy looks like a target path for the price level. It reduces 1) uncertainty about inflation at long horizons, 2) risk of deflation 3) confusion about the medium run stance of monetary policy and 4) the likelihood of asset pricing bubbles and other forms of economic instability. A well designed policy imposes little or no short run constraint on the Central Bank's use of discretion to manage economic risks. Instead, such a policy removes some risks and enhances the central banks ability to deal with those that remain. (Gavin 2003).

7. An inflation-targeting strategy also avoids several of the problems arising from monetary targeting or fixed exchange rate strategies. For example, in contrast to a fixed exchange rate system, inflation targeting can preserve a country's independent monetary policy so that the monetary authorities can cope with domestic shocks and help insulate the domestic economy from foreign shocks. In addition, inflation targeting can avoid the problem presented by velocity shocks because it eliminates the need to focus on the link between a monetary aggregate and nominal income; instead, all relevant information may be brought to bear on forecasting inflation and choosing a policy response to achieve a desirable inflation outcome.

8. Inflation targeting as a monetary policy influences fiscal policy to be a disciplined one.

DISADVANTAGES, CONCERNS OR MISCONCEPTIONS OF INFLATION TARGETING

1. According to Mishkin (1997), it is far harder for policy makers to hit on Inflation target with precision than it is for them to fix the exchange rate or achieve a monetary aggregate target. Furthermore, because the lags of the effect of monetary policy on Inflation are very long (typical estimates are in excess of two years in industrialized countries) much time must pass before a country can evaluate the success of monetary policy in achieving its inflation target. This problem does not arise with either a fixed exchange rate regime or a monetary aggregate target.

2. Another potential disadvantage is that, it may be taken literally as a rule that precludes any concern with output stabilization. (Mishkin et al 1997).

3. Chairman Bernanke (Bernanke, 2003) states as a misconception—that inflation targeting is inconsistent with Central Bank's obligation to maintain financial stability.

4. Kohn (2003) objects to inflation targeting because it might constrain a Central Bank's abilities in changing conditions.
5. True stable inflation target rate of zero does not give room for growth but prospects deflation.

CASE STUDIES

Case Study 1: Mishkin, F, and Posen A., "Inflation Targeting. Lessons from four countries"

—New Zealand, Canada, United Kingdom and Germany. (August 1997)

CASE STUDY CONCLUSION

"Our assessment of the effectiveness of inflation targeting in New Zealand, Canada, and the United Kingdom is on the whole positive. In all three countries, the adoption of targets was followed by the movement of inflation into, and the maintenance of inflation within, the announced target range. In the time since the adoption of inflation targets, our unconditional forecasts indicate that inflation and nominal interest rates have remained low in all three countries relative to the amount of output growth seen (which itself approximates the level forecast). This set of results is consistent with the interpretation that inflation does not appear to rise with business cycle expansions as it had in the past."(Mishkin et al, 1997).

Case Study 2: B.S Bernanke, T. Laubach, F.S. Mishkin, and A. S. Posen. 1998. "Inflation Targeting: Lessons from the

International Experience"—New Zealand, Canada, United Kingdom, Sweden, Israel, Australia and Spain.

CASE STUDY CONCLUSION

"The record of inflation targeting is good, albeit short at this point. There is strong evidence that inflation and inflation expectations have both fallen and become more stable in inflation targeting countries. In particular, it appears that inflation, once down, stays down; there is less tendency for inflation to rise during business cycle expansions. Low and stable inflation should promote growth and output stability in the long run. However, as already noted, the hope that inflation targeting might reduce the output costs of an initial disinflation does not appear to have been borne out". (Bernanke et al, 1998)

Case Study 3: Dotsey, M., A Review of Inflation Targeting in developed countries (2006)—New Zealand, Canada, Australia, United Kingdom.

CASE STUDY CONCLUSION

"A number of countries have implemental inflation targeting, and it has been in effect in a few of these countries for more than 10 years. The exact nature of the inflation-targeting framework differs across countries, and in most countries, it has evolved over time. As expressed in their testimony and speeches, monetary policymakers in the five inflation-targeting Countries examined in this article all seem to be pleased with the results and have found the framework flexible enough to allow consideration of economic performance. There is no indication that inflation targeting has diminished economic performance in countries that have adopted it relative to the performance of other industrialized countries. Indeed, there is some evidence that inflation targeting has been associated with a reduction in inflation and that expectations of inflation are more stable in countries that have adopted inflation targeting. Further, inflation targeting appears to be compatible with robust economic activity.

While the empirical evidence on the effects of inflation targeting is encouraging, we must acknowledge that the data that lend themselves to this optimistic view are limited. The experiment of inflation targeting has proceeded for a fairly short time, and thus, it has probably not been subject to all the vagaries that economies can experience. However, the testimony of central bankers who have been responsible for guiding monetary policy in the five inflation-targeting countries has been overwhelmingly positive. Many cannot envision departing from their current practices and returning to regimes that were less explicit about underlying inflation goals. They point to numerous instances where having an inflation target both focused monetary policy and made it easier to conduct". (Dotsey, 2006). Refer to Table 2 for data.

TABLE 2

Inflation and output growth in inflation-targeting countries, before and After

Country	Pre-inflation Targeting (10 years prior to Adopting target; for dates see Table 1)				Post-inflation Targeting-2004 (for dates see Table 1)			
	inflation	growth	s.d. inflation	s. d. growth	inflation	growth	s. d. inflation	s. d. growth
NZ	11.4	1.8	2.9	2.7	2.1	3.0	1.8	2.4
Canada	5.7	2.8	2.9	2.9	2.0	2.7	1.3	2.1
U. K.	5.5	2.5	3.0	1.9	2.5	2.9	0.8	0.7
Australia	6.0	3.2	2.9	2.7	2.6	3.8	1.6	1.1
Sweden	6.7	1.9	2.9	2.3	1.5	2.5	1.1	1.6
Avg. IT	7.1	2.4	2.9	2.5	2.1	3.0	1.3	1.6

Inflation and output growth in nomination-targeting countries, comparison

	1982-1992				1992-2004			
	inflation	growth	s.d. inflation	s. d. growth	inflation	growth	s. d. inflation	s. d. growth
NZ	11.4	1.8	2.9	2.7	2.1	3.0	1.8	2.4
U. S.	4.0	3.0	1.3	2.6	2.5	3.3	0.6	1.2
Japan	1.9	3.7	1.1	1.8	0.1	1.1	1.0	1.6
Germany	2.6	2.7	1.7	5.3	1.8	1.1	1.4	1.4
France	5.1	2.2	3.3	1.1	1.6	1.9	0.6	1.3
Neth.	2.6	2.5	2.3	2.2	2.4	2.4	0.8	1.6
Italy	8.3	2.2	4.6	1.3	3.0	1.5	1.3	1.4
Avg. NIT	4.1	2.7	2.4	2.4	1.9	1.9	1.0	1.4

Inflation rates are annualized changes in the headline CPI and growth rates are annualized rates of growth in GDP

Source: Dotsey (2006)

CHAPTER FOUR

ANALYSIS AND CONCLUSION

Inflation from the foregoing can be said to be a rise of average prices through the economy. It also means that the underlying cause is usually too much money is available to purchase too few gods and services, or that demand in the economy is outpacing supply. In general, this situation occurs when an economy is so buoyant that there are widespread shortages of labor and materials. People can charge higher prices for the same goods or services.

Inflation can also be caused by a rise in the prices of imported commodities, such as oil. However, this sort of inflation is usually transient, and less crucial than the structural inflation caused by an over-supply of money.

Inflation can be very damaging for a number of reasons. First, people may be left worse off if prices rise faster than their incomes. Second, inflation can reduce the value of an investment if the returns prove insufficient to compensate them for inflation. Third, since bouts of inflation often go hand in hand with an overheated economy, they can accentuate boom-bust cycles in the economy.

Sustained inflation also has longer-term effects. If money is losing its value, businesses and investors are less likely to make long-term contracts. This discourages long-term investment in the nation's productive capacity.

The flip-side of inflation is deflation. This occurs when average prices are falling, and can also result in various economic effects. For example, people will put off spending it they expect prices to fall. Sustained deflation can cause a rapid economic slow-down.

There are various ways of measuring inflation, but the most widely used is the consumer price Index, however its limitation. Since 2000 the Federal Reserve uses the core PCE price index. It claims, is more accurate and consistent in measuring and predicting inflation over the consumer Price Index. The core PCE makes room for hedonic adjustments and exclude volatile goods like energy and food products. Some critics however say this is conflict of interest for the Federal Reserve since some government income stabilization commitments are inflation indexed e.g. social security, welfare payments etc., so the government benefits from using the core PCE index which is usually lower than the general CPI.

In view of the inequities, anxieties, real losses and social pathologies caused by inflation it is not surprising that **price stability** is a major monetary policy goal of most industrialized countries including the United States. In pursuit of price stability many countries have debated the merits of inflation targeting, and some have adopted inflation targeting as a national policy. In inflation-targeting framework, a central bank announces quantitative targets for inflation and specifies that controlling inflation is a long-run goal of monetary policy. Another common feature is a specific policy for bringing inflation back to target in circumstances where the target has been missed. Also, inflation-targeting central banks have often adopted a more transparent policy that entails fairly detailed communications with the public.

New Zealand first instituted this monetary policy framework in early 1990. Since that time, 22 countries have formally adopted inflation targeting, and no country that has adopted it has abandoned it. (Dotsey, 2006)

Although inflation targeting contribution to overall economic performance is still being debated, the general view is that it has had beneficial effects. Inflation and its volatility have generally declined in inflation-targeting countries and output growth has increased. At the same time, it appears that the volatility of output has decreased.

Why did these countries choose inflation targeting over alternative policy frameworks? First, the authorities in these countries had decided that achieving price stability—a low and steady inflation rate-is the major contribution that monetary policy can make to economic growth. Second, practical experience has demonstrated that short-term manipulation of monetary policy to achieve other goals—higher employment or perhaps enhanced output-may conflict with price stability. Some economists believe that an attempt to achieve several economic goals gives monetary policy an inflationary bias. Central Banks certainly appear to get more public criticism for raising interest rates (a customary anti-inflationary tactic) than for lowering them, and they are subject to constant pressure to stimulate economic activity. Also, as learned from Mishkin (1997) many central banks are choosing inflation targeting due to the invalidation of the Phillips inflation employment tradeoff hypothesis by Milton Friedman and Phelps, the inability of monetary aggregates to show any stable relationship with nominal income and inflation, the problems associated with targeting exchange rates and the time inconsistency issues with activist monetary policy. Inflation targeting in principle helps redress this asymmetry by making inflation—rather than employment, output, or some other criterion—the primary goal of monetary policy. It also forces the central bank to look ahead, giving it the opportunity to tighten policies before inflation pressures become intense.

Inflation targeting is straightforward, at least in theory. The central bank forecasts the future path of inflation; the forecast is compared with the target inflation rate (the inflation rate the government believes appropriate for the economy); the difference between the forecast and the target determines how much monetary policy has to be adjusted. Countries that have adopted inflation targeting believe it can improve the design and performance of monetary policy compared with conventional procedures followed by central banks.

The focus on the inflation rate highlights the paramount role that inflation forecasts play in this approach. Since the forecast dictates how monetary policy should respond, the structure of the economy must be stable and easily modeled to ensure an accurate forecast.

The definition of the inflation target also varies across the countries studied. The main difference concerns the time horizon specified (how long it would take to reach the goal and how long the target would prevail), how the price level is measured, and whether the target was specified in terms of a point or a band.

Biases in the calculation of the CPI (owing, for example, to the introduction of new goods or to higher demand for better-quality goods, new labor wage contracts) imply that, in practice, price stability is likely to be associated with a small positive rate of CPI inflation rather than a zero rate. These and other considerations have caused the inflation targets to center on a rate of about 2 percent a year. At such low levels, targeting an even low inflation rate is unlikely, according to existing empirical evidence, to yield significant benefits.

A major difference in the definition of inflation targets across countries was the width of the band around the central target. In Canada, U.K and Sweden, the framework focused on a particular point target for the inflation rate, New Zealand and Australia specified a range for the inflation target.

The need to specify a bandwidth results from the imperfect control of monetary policy over the inflation rate. The choice of a bandwidth reflects a trade-off between announcing a tight, hard-edged band, which may occasionally be breached, and announcing a wide band, which may be regarded as "softness" on the part of the central bank. Market participants may interpret a narrower band as indicating a stronger commitment to the inflation target. If remaining inside a narrow band proves, difficult in practice, however, frequent breaches could undermine any credibility gain.

The merits enumerated in this book for inflation targeting clearly outweighs the demerits or disadvantages. Some critics of inflation have argued that the approach is not appealing because of the time that it takes monetary policy action to affect inflation, as well as the difficulties of forecasting inflation. These concerns are cited as reason for policy to target intermediate targets such as monetary aggregates, exchanges rates or other variables that can be more directly controlled than prices. These arguments are rather illogical because they are inconsistent with the management model of "Management by Objective". The issue is that either the proposed intermediate targets bear a stable relationship to long-run objective like inflation or they do not. If they do not bear any stable relationship to long run-objective, then there is no reason for targeting them. As stated, supra, the conventional intermediate targets did not have any stable relationship with price stability hence the apparent drift to inflation targeting by countries currently practicing it and other countries being influenced by the framework including the United States. The current chairman of the Federal Reserve Board is a major advocate of the Inflation targeting framework. The fact that Inflation targeting regimes are becoming successful means that the various econometric models applied in forecasting are reasonably working well. I have no doubt that with time, it will be more perfected to the point that most Central Banks will be right on target.

Another concern that inflation targeting may be taken literally as a rule that precludes any concern with output stabilization and the Central Bank ability to affect short run conditions is rather a misconception. To start with, this has not happened in practice. It is fundamentally incorrect to characterize inflation targeting (as conducted in practice) as an ironclad policy rule, in the sense of the traditional rules-versus-discretion debate. Instead, inflation targeting is better thought of as a policy framework, in which policy is "tied down" against the long run in which there is target (which serves as a nominal anchor for the system), but in which there is also considerable leeway for policymakers to pursue other objectives in the short run. In particular, adoption of inflation targeting does not amount to abandoning output stabilization. First, inflation targeting, even in the short run, is consistent with stabilization output against aggregate demand shocks. Second, negative supply shocks can be handled within the inflation targeting framework by various mechanisms, such as the hedonic adjustments or exclusion of volatile components from the targeted price index. Another option is lengthening the period over which the inflation target is to be reached. In best practice inflation targeting connotes flexibility therefore inflation targeting permits a degree of policy discretion in the short run, allowing the central bank to respond to current economic developments, so long as the long-run inflation goal is not compromised.

Achieving a degree of short-run flexibility for policy requires that the public's expectations of inflation remain stable in the face of short-run fluctuations in policy and the economy. In other words, the medium-and long-term inflation goals of the central bank must be reasonably credible. In practice, inflation-targeting central banks have sought to strengthen their credibility by taking measures to increase transparency and accountability. Transparency requires that policymakers' objectives, information, and plans be communicated clearly and in a regular and timely fashion to the government and the public. All inflation targeting central banks have taken substantial steps towards openness in policymaking, for example through regular publication of inflation reports that include detailed information on inflation prospects and likely policy responses or statements outlining the "balance of risks" in the future, whether toward higher inflation or a weaker economy. Accountability requires at a minimum that the central bank stake its reputation on either meeting its inflation targets or in providing clear and compelling reasons for why the target was missed.

The argument that inflation targeting is inconsistent with Central Bank's obligation to maintain financial stability is no argument but a misconception. The concept of inflation targeting is a conservative one that requires the preservation of financial stability. Thus, the framework provides for liquidity at low rates and a stable economic environment for better liability, Asset, Liquidity and Capital Management.

Empirical evidence rendered from the three case studies used in this research affirms the successes of inflation targeting. Mervyn King (2003) the governor of the Bank of England said the following regarding their success with inflation targeting: "Only since 1992 has inflation been consistently below 4 percent, and in fact it has averaged a fraction under 2.5 percent of our target for the past ten years with growth averaging 25 percent a year and a little above the historical trend. Inflation has been low and stable. Unemployment came down from double digit levels to 5 percent. And there have been forty-two consecutive quarters of positive economic growth, which I think is unprecedented, at least in our history". He made this remark in his submission during the Inflation targeting debate convened by the National Bureau of Economic Research in Miami, Florida (January 2003). The U.K adopted Inflation Targeting Monetary Policy in October 1992. Prior to 1992, according to Mervyn King, the U.K. had "great inflation" in which inflation peaked at 27 percent in the mid 1970s and averaged 13 percent a year right through the whole of that decade. It averaged over 7 percent a year through the 1980s under Mrs. Thatcher.

The advantages of inflation targeting have been so convincing that many central banks that have not formally adopted the framework of inflation targeting have clearly been influenced by the approach or framework. For example, over the past twenty years, the Federal Reserve, even though, not a formal inflation targeting regime has been implementing the framework. It has greatly increased its credibility for maintaining low and stable inflation and has become more proactive in heading off inflationary pressures and improved the transparency of its policy making process. Also, in the survey of five industrialized inflation targeting countries, Truman (2003) finds that industrialized inflation-targeting countries experience both an increase in output growth and a reduction in output volatility relative to the experience of non-inflation targeting countries. Table 2 depicts the data on Inflation and output Growth in Inflation Targeting and non-inflation targeting countries, before and after.

The inflation target announced increases the effectiveness of Monetary Policy. It not only guides households and business in price and wage decision making but also provides a yardstick against which Central Bank actions may be judged. Under this framework Central Bank authorities can be asked to justify or be accountable for their monetary policy decisions. In New Zealand and the U.K for example, the Central Bank governors must explain to their Minister or the Chancellor of the Exchequer why they missed target. In New Zealand the governor is personally accountable for its monetary policy success. The Central Bank governor is by law required to enter into a Policy Target Agreement with the Minister of Finance committing the Governor to meet the legal target within specified times. The policy target agreement is then made public. Any changes to be made in the Policy Target Agreement should be initiated by the government and be made public and a new agreement to be renegotiated with the governor. This measure gives the central bank a great measure of independence. The New Zealand Central Bank is said to have been transformed from one of the least independent Central Bank to one of the most independent Central Banks among developed countries as a result of implementing the inflation targeting framework through an act in 1989 but came into force in 1990.(Mishkin, 2002) .

The institutional arrangement features towards the commitment to an inflation target in the Inflation targeting framework is what makes me proffer that Inflation targeting enhances the effectiveness of Monetary Policy. The inflation targeting framework for me is a 'checks and balances' approach to Monetary Policy commission. It makes Central Banking independent as a check on government intrusion yet responsible. It is 'triangular' in nature that is Policy Formulation, Implementation and Accounting.

(PIA TRIANGLE)

POLICY FORMULATION

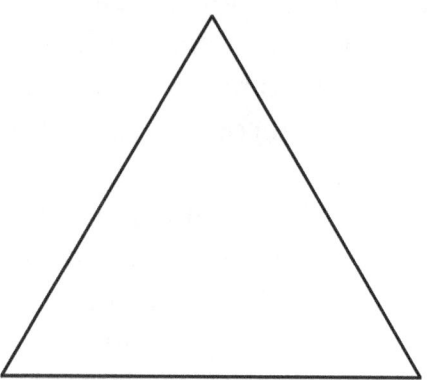

IMPLEMENTATION   ACCOUNTING

The Policy formulation represents the Central Bank establishing numerical objectives that are to be met over specified periods. The Implementation represents announcing the numerical objectives to the public, implementing monetary policy tools, typically influencing cash rate or inter-bank lending rates through open market operations, and targeting the desired price level measure, that is either the headline Consumer Price Index or the Core Price Index. The Policy Accounting involves the Publication of Inflation target report that explains to the public at large whether target was met or otherwise and reasons for any misses. The report must also include information on inflation prospects, likely policy responses and a "balance of risks" statement against the future. To make the inflation targeting model work better I propose that the committee that does the policy formulation sign off the inflation report assuming responsibilities and liabilities.

I also posit that all Central Bank governors sign a covenant with the people through the government to not only to commit to and achieve target but also make the Central Bank liable for damages should they miss target beyond tolerance. Various law making bodies should accordingly pass laws giving individuals and businesses 'standing' to sue the policy making committee and the central bank jointly and or severally for damages proximately caused from the reliance on the inflation target commitments put out by Central Banks. This way public expectation of inflation will be very well anchored while the Central Bank is made responsible. In reverse, Central Bank governors should be specially rewarded for meeting targets. This way they have the incentive to achieve.

Theory has it that nominal interest rate is determined by adding real interest rate plus anticipated rate of inflation or current inflation rate plus premiums.(Schiller, 2003). One is therefore likely to find relatively low interest rates in low inflation economies than high inflation economies. The Keynesian investment function in Macro-economics posits that there is a lower rate of investment spending when interest rates are high and more investment spending when interest rates are low, therefore in a low inflation environment as a result of inflation targeting, there should be more consumption by households and businesses because money is cheaper and the future price path level picture is clear. This means investors will borrow to produce to sustain aggregate demand which involves increased utilization of labor, meaning a reduction in Unemployment or increased Employment, hence my thesis; "Inflation targeting as a Monetary Policy not only enhances the effectiveness of Monetary Policy but also stabilizes rate of inflation, economic growth and employment." *Ceteris Paribus.*

REFERENCES

1. Anderson John Ward. 1999. "Tortilla Price Hikes Hits Mexico's Poorest". Washington Post. 12 Jan 1999, 44-45

2. *Bank of Canada:* www. Bankofcanada.ca

3. *Bank. of England*: www. bankofengland.com

4. Baumol, William J. and Alan S. Blinder. 2006. *Macroeconomics: Principles and Policy*, 10th Edition. Thomas South Western

5. Bernanke Ben S. and Michael Woodford. 2003. *The Inflation Targeting Debate*. The University Of Chicago Press.

6. Bernanke, B.S., T. Laubach, F.S Mishkin and A.S Posen. 1999. *Inflation Targeting: Lessons Form International Experience*. Princeton: Princeton University Press

7. Bernanke, B.S., 2003 "A Perspective on Inflation Targeting". Remarks at the Annual Washington Policy Conference of the National Association of Business Economist: FRB New York.

8. Bernanke, Ben S. and Frederic S. Mishkin. 1992 "Central Bank Behavior and the Strategy of Monetary Policy: Observation Form Six Industrialized Countries" *NBER Macroeconomics Annual*. Cambridge: MIT Press.

9. Case Karl E. and Ray C. Fair. 2004. *Principles of Macroeconomics*. Boston Addison Wesley.

10. *Consumer Price Index*. Stats.bls.gov/cpi

11. Dostey, Mike. 2006 "A Review of Inflation Targeting in Developed Countries": www.philadelphia.org. Business Review Q3 2006.

12. Feldstein, Martin.1997. "The Costs and Benefit Of Going Form Low Inflation To Price Stability" In Christian D. Roma And David H. Romer, eds., REDUCING INFLATION; MOTIVATION AND STRATEGY Inflation: 123-56. Chicago: University Of Chicago Press.

13. Fischer, Stanley. 1981. "Towards an Understanding of Costs of Inflation: II." Carnegie-Rochester Conference Series On Public Policy 15:5-41

14. Gavin, Williams T. 2003. "Inflation Targeting: Why it works and how to make it work better." Working Paper Series, FRB of St. Louis: September 2003-027b.

15. Greenspan, Allen. 1988. *Statement before the committee on Banking, Finance, and Urban Affairs, U.S. Senate.*

16. Groshen, Eric L, Schweitzer. 1996."*The Effects Of Inflation On Wage Adjustments In Firm-Level Data:*

Grease Or Sand? Fergal Reserve Bank Of New York Staff Reports, No. 9

17. King, Mervyn. 2003. "What has Inflation Targeting Achieved? *The Inflation Targeting Debate*. Chicago. The University Of Chicago Press.

18. McCallum, Bennett T. 1995. "Two Fallacies Concerning Central Bank Independence". *American Economic Review* 85 , No. 2 (May) : 207-11

19. Mishkin, Frederic 1996. *"Understanding Financial Crisis : A Developing Country Perspective"*. Annual World Bank Conference On Development Economics 29-62,Washington D.C: World Bank

20. Mishkin, F, Posen A, "Inflation Targeting :Lessons From Four Countries" *Economic Policy Review*, Federal Reserve Bank Of New York, 3 (August 1997), 9-110

21. Mishkin, Frederic. 2002, *Financial Market + Institutions*. Boston Addison Wesley.

22. Mishkin Frederic S., 2007. "Monetary Policy and Dual Mandate". Remarks by Governor Frederic S. Mishkin At Bridgewater College, April 2007

23. Murray N. Rothbard. *What Has Government Done To Our Money?* ISBN 0945466447

24. Okun,Arthur.1978.'Real Cost of Inflation". *Business Week.* 22 May 1978, p.46

25. Riesman, George. 1990: *A Treatise On Economics*. Ottawa. Jameson Books

26. Royal Bank of New Zealand. www.rbnz.govt.nz

27. *Worldwide Inflation*. w.ww.imf.org

28. *Reserve Bank of Australia*. www.rba.gov.au

29. Rose, Marquis.200. *Money and Capital Markets*. McGraw Hill

30. Schiller, Bradley R. 2003. *The Economy Today*. Boston McGraw Hill

31. Shapiro, Matthew D., and David W. Wilcox. 1996. "Causes and Consequences of Imperfections in the Consumer Price Index." *NBER Macroeconomic Annual*, Cambridge: MIT Press.

32. Svensson, Lars E. O and Michael Woodford.2003. "Implementing Optimal Policy through Inflation-Forecast targeting." *The Inflation Targeting Debate*. Chicago. The University of Chicago Press.

33. Taylor, John B. 1993. *"Discretion Versus Policy Rules in Practice"* Carnegie-Rochester Conference Series on Public Policy". 39,195-214

34. Rogoff Kenneth. 1985. "The Optimal Commitment to an Intermediate Monetary Target". *Quarterly Journal of Economics*. No. 100

www.ingramcontent.com/pod-product-compliance
Lightning Source LLC
Chambersburg PA
CBHW031246280526
45784CB00004B/1736